SPRING GROVE

SPRING GROVE

THE EDUCATION OF IMMIGRANT CHILDREN

TREVOR BURGIN

AND

PATRICIA EDSON

Published for the
Institute of Race Relations, London
OXFORD UNIVERSITY PRESS
LONDON   NEW YORK

Oxford University Press, Ely House, London W.1

GLASGOW NEW YORK TORONTO MELBOURNE WELLINGTON
CAPE TOWN SALISBURY IBADAN NAIROBI DAR ES SALAAM LUSAKA ADDIS ABABA
BOMBAY CALCUTTA MADRAS KARACHI LAHORE DACCA
KUALA LUMPUR SINGAPORE HONG KONG TOKYO

SBN 19 218189 0

First published 1967
Reprinted 1970

PRINTED IN GREAT BRITAIN BY
BUTLER AND TANNER LTD, FROME AND LONDON

CONTENTS

PREFACE TO THE SECOND IMPRESSION

Since the original manuscript of this book was completed early in 1966, much positive action has taken place, and progress has been made in the education of children from overseas at both local and national levels. In Huddersfield immigrant children have continued to arrive from Asia and the Caribbean, and the swelling of numbers of immigrant pupils, together with the rise in proportion of children born each year to parents from overseas, led the local education authority to re-design its approach.

Whilst it was felt that the system of special English classes within an ordinary school provided the most satisfactory answer to the needs of non-English-speaking children, increasing pressure of numbers indicated that Spring Grove itself would no longer be able to cope alone. It was therefore decided to initiate similar schemes at a number of other schools in the town at both primary and secondary levels. Consequently as many as 26 schools now run one, two, or three special English classes which function on extremely similar lines to the ones described in this book, with the children being integrated into normal classes as soon as they are able to hold their own. In this way it is hoped that much of what has been developed and achieved at Spring Grove will carry over into many more schools, at the same time ensuring that each school will have a racially well-balanced population.

Prior to their dispersal into appropriate schools, all children of Asiatic origin attend a Reception for four to six weeks, where they can spend a short period of acclimatization in a relaxed atmosphere, becoming accustomed to English school routine, and adjusting themselves to a variety of new experiences. At the same time they undergo a medical examination and are given essential social and road safety training by a team of experienced teachers. These teachers, both English and Asiatic, are able to assess the linguistic needs of the children, at the same time providing them with a feeling of security while they come to terms with their new surroundings.

Children from the Caribbean are placed in neighbourhood or near-neighbourhood schools, and where additional help in language and basic subjects is found to be necessary, a team of peripatetic teachers, under the guidance of the senior remedial teacher, is able to provide skilled service in this direction.

At national level, various steps have been taken to meet the increasing demands made by the newcomers from overseas and to help teachers who are being faced with these children, possibly for the first time. The advisory committee on education of the Community Relations Commission (formerly the N.C.C.I.) has attempted to deal with aspects of curriculum development, post-school education, advice to L.E.A.s, but probably the most encouraging results have emanated from their attempt to initiate a sense of urgency into the re-orientation of courses in colleges of education. The Schools Councils have inaugurated two projects at the universities of Leeds and Birmingham to investigate and produce material relevant to the needs of non-English-speaking and West Indian children, respectively, and the first of these, under the title of SCOPE, is already in use in many multi-racial classrooms. The formation of an increasing number of local branches of the Association of Teachers of English to Pupils from Overseas (ATEPO) and the establishment of their national federation have ensured that the teachers themselves are keenly aware of the role they themselves have to play. Many areas, including Huddersfield, have appointed experienced people to posts of responsibility and coordination as advisers or organizers.

Finally, the courses being made available locally as integral features of in-service training have been complemented at national level by the Department of Education and Science through a series of conferences on second-language teaching techniques, the background of immigrants, books and equipment, and the education of young children in multi-racial classrooms. However, despite what has taken place so far, we feel that there are still challenges being presented by the ever-changing patterns of our classrooms and trust that what is contained in this book will continue to serve as an encouragement and guide to those willing to meet these challenges.

T. Burgin
P. Edson

1970

FOREWORD BY J. P. W. MALLALIEU

Over the centuries, people of many different races have settled in Britain.

We derive much of our strength and world-wide influence from this fact.

But each successive wave of immigrants has brought with it severe problems of assimilation. We are finding this in our times with the wave of immigration which began around 1950.

The proper integration into our national life of the Continental, African, West Indian, and Asian immigrants who have come here in recent years is indeed one of the major social issues of today.

Mr. Trevor Burgin and his staff at Spring Grove County School, Huddersfield, have made a serious contribution to the solution of this problem.

The methods they have used to lead both the immigrant children and their parents into our way of life are being studied and copied by education authorities all over the country; and this book gives a full and absorbing account of their work.

Mr. Burgin and Mrs. Edson know better than I do that the problem is not yet solved. But the book repeats a lesson, which the history of these islands has already taught, that the problem is not insoluble.

I hope that everyone who is concerned about race relations in Britain today will read it.

J. P. W. MALLALIEU
House of Commons, October 1965

ACKNOWLEDGEMENTS

We should like to express our gratitude to Mr. J. P. W. Mallalieu, M.P., for his foresight, interest, and encouragement, and to Mr. Christopher Hill, Mr. Simon Abbott and Miss Claire Pace, of the Institute of Race Relations, for their helpful comments and criticisms.

We are indebted to Mr. Keith Pickup, former Educational Psychologist for Huddersfield, for his assistance with the chapter on testing, and to Mrs. M. Firth and Mrs. W. Moorhouse for their invaluable secretarial help.

Finally, we are indeed grateful to Mrs. A. J. Massey, Head of the Special English Department, Spring Grove Primary School, to Miss A. H. Blatch, her predecessor, and to all present and former members of the staff of Spring Grove School without whose enthusiasm and unfailing good humour this experiment could not have taken place.

T. Burgin
P. Edson

CHAPTER I

PRELUDE

Spring Grove School stands on a windswept ridge overlooking the industrial Colne Valley. Almost as far as the eye can see, closely packed grey terraced houses jostle together in a jungle of mill chimneys, while beyond the pall of soot and smoke, not too far distant, the bare moorland hills, sometimes snow-capped, roll into the horizon.

Many of our pupils live in the busy grey community below, and wind their way laboriously to school each day up the steep 'cat-steps' which lead to the playground.

On the other three sides, the school is flanked by more rows of decaying, soot-covered terraced houses, joined by quiet cobbled streets, the continuity broken occasionally by a tiny church or a Pakistani grocer's shop. More dramatically, within fifty yards of the school, there rises unexpectedly out of the middle of the road a vast round chimney, a railway ventilation shaft, which emits clouds of black smoke from the tunnel below at intervals throughout the day. Behind it, an Indian shop, also doing duty as an off-licence, advertises the local ale, and, at the same time, the forthcoming programme of the Pakistani Film Society. It smells pungently of spices and Indian sweet-meats. Next door, exotic sari lengths of brightly coloured silk interwoven with silver filigree, mingle for sale, uncomplainingly, with pairs of black, knee-length working boots.

This quiet, grey island between the elegant Greenhead Park and the busy town centre has seen better days. Nowadays the buildings are obviously dying, and occasionally rat-infested. Many are destined for slum clearance, and many more house large numbers of immigrant families. Pretty West Indian children play in the streets, and beautiful, dignified Indian women, still in their national dress, walk sedately between their homes and the shops.

Built in 1879, the school was revolutionary in its design, for

it allowed the education authorities to introduce something
long needed in schools—a separate classroom for each class.
This is something which we now automatically accept as a pre-
requisite in any educational establishment, but in those days it
replaced the method whereby several teachers and their classes
were accommodated together in a long hall. The passing of the
'aild shed' was greeted with much relief, when in 1880 the new
Spring Grove building was opened by the Vice-President of the
Committee of the Council on Education.

Within the building two storeys of classrooms surround the
main hall, the dominating feature of which is a tiered gallery
at one end, complete with a pulpit. The fact that all the classrooms open either directly on to the hall, or on to a balcony
which overlooks the hall on three sides, makes for an intimacy
and a feeling of family closeness which has proved invaluable
in a multiracial school.

This hall provides an ideal setting for choral and dramatic
presentations, as well as our daily morning assembly, and
naturally it is also used for many of the school's physical
activities. This to some extent compensates for the fact that, in
common with many schools in heavily built-up areas, we are
badly handicapped by the lack of adequate outdoor playing
facilities. Fortunately, this has not prevented the school from
taking part in football, cricket, netball, and rounders, owing to
the generosity of two local schools, which allow us to use their
playing fields, and to the fact that we are able to make use of the
nearby Greenhead Park.

Since the opening of the new building in 1880, both the
school and the area in which it is situated have undergone a
change of character which has reflected new social situations.
Once a fashionable residential area, the houses are now dis-
appearing into heaps of rubble and frequent bonfires of old
wood, slowly making way for the new Civic Centre. In the
meantime the ground so cleared has been newly surfaced to
accommodate the town's rapidly increasing number of cars.

Between the wars the larger houses in the area achieved a
reputation for being good lodging-places for members of the
theatrical profession who were engaged to perform in local
theatres. From 1929 the school admission registers show frequent entries of groups of thirteen-year-old children, who were

taking part in a production—often a pantomime. It is reasonable to assume that about 1930 there were increasing public demands for these young children to receive full-time education suitable to their age, ability, and aptitude, and the enforcement of the Children and Young Persons' Act of 1933 ensured that the children of people who wandered from place to place did actually attend school. However, their length of study within the Spring Grove walls was rarely more than a week, when they moved on to their next port of call. Prior to this time the responsibility had rested solely with each individual and so it was pleasing to note that one entry in the Log Book for April 1917 reads: 'Seven new scholars were admitted today, four of these for one week only, as they are engaged at the Palace Music Hall.' Often as many as a dozen at a time of these young stars were admitted, and have been known to attend school in Red Riding Hood capes and with long golden ringlets. Sometimes the children were not performers themselves, but the sons and daughters of circus people or fairground-proprietors who were spending a week in the town.

By the early 1950s our admission registers were beginning to take on an international flavour, as numbers of Poles, Yugoslavs, Ukrainians, and Latvians were coming to live in the area. As often happens with town-centre dwellings, the houses were reasonably priced in comparison with the now more fashionable and 'desirable' suburbs, and immigrants in more straitened financial circumstances found in them an adequate, yet cheap, home. Once established economically these European immigrants moved to more attractive areas, and for the same economic reasons, Indians, Pakistanis, and West Indians began to take over the property.

It was from these varied ethnic groups that the seeds of our particular educational problem were sown, and our story is an attempt to tell how, within the school, we have tried to adapt our methods of teaching to a new social situation, in the same way that the houses and streets themselves have altered their character with each new wave of tenants.

CHAPTER II

PATTERNS OF IMMIGRANT ARRIVALS

The fact that in Huddersfield we have a comparatively high level of employment and an adequately varied selection of industries, has assured our immigrant population of a level of security and tolerance which, for various reasons, has not been forthcoming in all receiving towns and cities. Where work is scarce and housing difficult, racial discrimination and intolerance simmer barely beneath the surface, but where the man-in-the-street has no housing problem and feels economically secure, he is prepared to live and let live.

Among Huddersfield industries which make heavy demands for labour are wool textiles, textile machinery, dyeing, light and medium engineering, electric motors, foundries, the building industry and its sub-industries, and coal-mining. In addition, immigrants are able to provide an essential part of the labour force in the public services, in particular the borough transport department and British Railways. Local hospitals, also, are extremely well served both in quantity and quality at all levels by immigrant workers of both sexes; in fact it would probably be true to say that the hospitals could not function without this help. A fair proportion of the Indian and Pakistani men are skilled and semi-skilled operatives in the textile trade, where there are many opportunities for weavers, spinners, and menders. The West Indian males, however, seem to supply the great bulk of unskilled labour in heavy engineering, and they can be found in pipe-works, foundries, and machine shops.

Furthermore employers know that these immigrant workers are far more willing to work regular night shifts than their local counterparts, and in these prosperous days firms are making use of their services to the full. Our children are always telling us that their fathers sleep during the day, and socially it may be relevant to mention that night work means that one room can be sublet to one man during the day and another at night, when they are on different shifts.

By 1958 the nationalities of children enrolled at our school reflected the entry into the town during the previous five years of a variety of Central European families. The children could be divided into roughly three groups. First, there were children of 'straight' European marriages—that is with both parents being of the same nationality—Polish, Yugoslav, or Ukrainian. Secondly, some of the children were of 'mixed' European marriages, that is with perhaps a Lithuainian father and a German mother. And, lastly, there were those who had one English parent, the other coming from one of the Central European countries.

Of these groups, quite obviously the last presented us with virtually no problem at all, as the common language of the home was almost invariably English. Of the other two groups, the second usually evolved into a largely English-speaking family unit, since the father would need English for work and the children learned to speak English at school; thus English formed a common language between mother and father. It was the children of the first group, who heard little or no English spoken at home, who provided the nucleus of our Special English class. Most of the Central European immigrants in Huddersfield seem to have been accepted into the textile trade, whilst the remainder have been drawn into Imperial Chemical Industries or David Brown's, two of the largest industrial concerns in the area.

During recent years we have admitted several Italian children whose fathers have been craftsmen, and have come to this town with the specific purpose of working for a local firm of mosaic floor specialists. We have also taught the children of such varied tradespeople as Spanish hairdressers, Chinese restaurateurs, and Italian ice-cream vendors.

The late 1940s and 1950s saw a steady stream of Irish settlers, some of whom were wandering tinkers, for our area offered economic opportunity to the unskilled and semi-skilled. A number of the children spoke only Gaelic or Erse, so came into the category of non-English-speaking. Although many Irish pupils were accommodated in the town's Roman Catholic schools, Spring Grove, as the town-centre school serving the area in which these children lived, received more than its quota; before our Special English scheme started, those who did not speak English were put into a class usually much below their commensurate age group, and they were forced to struggle on as best they could.

Since the pressure on the town's two Roman Catholic schools has recently been relieved by the opening of two more large ones, almost all Irish children entering the borough are now able to attend schools of their own faith. Since 1958 we have received only one entirely non-English-speaking Irish girl, and she has now been transferred to an English-speaking class.

During the past six years, the character of the immigrant population has been enriched by the arrival of increasing numbers of Indians, Pakistanis, and West Indians. They have acquired houses in the town centre that were previously occupied by Europeans and Irish settlers, and now the Indians and Pakistanis provide by far the greatest number of pupils in our Special English department. The first settlers in any density of numbers were Indians from the Punjab, and the procedure when a child was enrolled at school always followed a definite pattern. Initially an Indian father would bring one child to be admitted, and this was invariably the eldest son. He would then bring his other children at intervals of three to four months. From this it was apparent that the father came to this country at the instigation of a relative or friend who vouched for the prospects locally, and then he sent for his family at appropriate stages as he achieved economic stability, with the mother being the last to leave the native home. This was the pattern from the very first arrival in 1956 until after 1960, when we noticed a change. Once the cultural group settlement had established a firm footing in Huddersfield, the Indians started to arrive as family units instead of one by one. Of course the mother could very rarely speak English, but our more advanced Special English children have always been most reliable as interpreters, and we always enjoy watching them cope with quick-fire translation between Punjabi and English.

Originally, when the father brought one of his children to school for admission, we managed without an interpreter, because the male's first need is always to learn the language of his new country in order to converse on public transport, in shops, and at his place of employment. Furthermore, he has always needed to accustom himself to our habits, laws, and regulations. A study of local population patterns in Huddersfield has shown the retention of family units, since many of our children are interrelated. Almost all our Indian children are Sikhs from the Punjab, and they are drawn almost without exception from a 'parish' area called Jullundur, not far from the West Pakistan border.

As the Indian community increased and as they were accepted, they gained a sense of group solidarity and started to establish their own shops, itinerant tradesmen, societies, and churches. The advantages of this cultural pluralism were many: guarantee of employment, help in the 'settling-down' process, assistance with accommodation, and the obvious opportunities to feel the new way of life while among others sharing similar problems of an unknown language, the strangeness of legal, religious, and political systems.

Our Pakistani intake to the school has reached large proportions only relatively recently, and the customary early reception pattern, as outlined for the Indian children, applies in a similar way, but if the intake continues at the high numerical rate of recent months, we have no doubt that the pattern will conform to type, and instead of a male Pakistani bringing Pakistani children (again mainly males) to school, we shall soon be having Pakistani mothers arriving complete with family.

We should greatly welcome this development, for it has been noticeable that in many Pakistani households the mother is conspicuous by her absence, and there is far too heavy a proportion of older males. These conditions invariably bring with them a crop of social problems, and throw a further responsibility for social integration on to the teachers, instead of its being shared with the parents. Any attempts at contact with the home environment during the day have usually resulted in our being told that the males were in bed, since they were on night work in the local factories and mills.

Huddersfield acts as a home base for Pakistanis who work at a nearby jute mill—a trade in which they can provide considerable expertise. The fact that wages, incentives, and conditions of work are the same for all workers, irrespective of creed or colour, is obviously a great attraction to these people, who are still entering the town regularly in large numbers. During the eight weeks before Christmas 1963, we admitted seventy-two non-English-speaking children, which was five more than in any one school year, and of these forty-two were Pakistanis.

In Huddersfield, while the Indian Sikhs come from Jullundur, the Pakistanis come mainly from Lyallpur, in West Pakistan. On occasions Karachi is given as the last address, but it is reasonable to assume that this has been their point of embarkation.

West Indian immigrants in the area come mainly from Jamaica and Grenada, with only very few from the other West Indian islands. Only in recent years have the West Indians tended to arrive in family groups, although they still seem to be the community providing the largest proportion of single males.

The fact that more married men with families are coming is reflected in their attitude to work on arrival. In the early days it was noticed at the employment exchange that when West Indians signed on, their first anxiety was not for labour, but how to apply for national assistance. Indians and Pakistanis, on the other hand, invariably asked: 'You have work for me, yes?' and wished to start as quickly as possible. But now the West Indians, mindful of their responsibilities, take the more normal approach for work. Their 'easy-come, easy-go' nature where work is concerned is partly a national trait, and partly due to a conditioning which seasonal work at home, leavened by what assistance they can muster in between, has inflicted. With the increase in England of more family units, however, there is a much greater need and desire for work. The Indians and Pakistanis, whether married or single, have been accustomed over the centuries to work hard with little hope of reward. In their families the male is always the family breadwinner, whereas in the West Indies the role is often undertaken by the womenfolk.

Mounting enrolments of West Indian children in the main school indicate a change in the balance of coloured children to white. In the present reception class, approximately one half of the children are West Indian, reflecting a review we made of the situation in 1961, noting that: 'Many of the West Indian children are not yet of school age, and can be seen playing in the streets surrounding the school.' Presumably, these children are now in school, and the high fertility rate among West Indian families would seem to suggest that we shall soon admit English-born West Indian children in greater proportion than the children of any other single ethnic group in the town.

Group settlement patterns, or 'chain migration', are reflected all over this country, as well as internationally, and examples can be found in many areas. In Bedfordshire for instance, there is a large community of Italian farm-workers, and in North London, Cypriots present the Education Authorities with a problem similar to that which we are tackling at Spring Grove. A survey conducted by Mr. Peter Wingard of Manchester University, into the cultural background of Indian children attending Bolton schools, indicated that 90 per cent of them were Muslims from the Bombay State area. This illustrates the fact that a community from a particular area of India has settled in one area of England, whilst another has become similarly uprooted, and resettled in another area—with the chosen area for each community being dependent on the choice of the first few pioneer immigrant families.

Examples of chain migration much farther afield can be seen in the Chinese communities in San Francisco and Vancouver. Likewise the French settlement in New Orleans and the Dutch community of Holland, in Michigan, are long-established and maintain much of the culture and languages of the first early settlers.

Also, in the same way that economic opportunity has attracted vast numbers of Indians and Pakistanis to the North of England, Puerto Ricans have been drawn to the American mainland, and their large community in New York presents a situation very similar to that in the Huddersfield area.

Although these patterns of group settlement have many advantages, one of the greatest obstacles to the mastery of the language of the receiving country is the tendency of the married women immigrants, who are mainly concerned with affairs of the home, to cling to their native tongue and to encourage its use in the home.

This we must accept and, as is the case in all host countries, we must realize that complete linguistic integration will not be achieved until the second generation at the earliest. Both males and females of the first generation will maintain contact with areas of origin by letter and by the spoken and written language.

This retention of the mother tongue has, from the very beginning, been a most noticeable feature of nearly all the non-English-speaking families whose children attend our school. Those from Poland, Lithuania, or the Ukraine, where both parents spoke the same language, tended to preserve their ethnic group settlements, their culture, and their language as much as possible, with the mother tongue being used all the time.

When a Ukrainian boy was admitted to school at five years of age, he could not speak any English, and when his younger brother was admitted three years later, he too was unable to utter more than a few words of our language. The younger brother had been born in the same house as the one in which the elder lived when he started school, and he has obviously lived his first five years very much confined within the family group, although the house is in no way isolated, being one of a row of terraced houses in the built-up area of the town centre.

Both of these children, fortunately, are intelligent and will not suffer, the older one having been selected for a local Grammar school. However, the average or less than average child would probably be held back by this sort of situation, as was another Ukrainian, whose work was somewhat retarded by his natural inclination to translate into Ukrainian and then back into English.

On the whole it seems evident that immigrants into Huddersfield, of the three major ethnic groups (that is, Indians, Pakistanis, and West Indians) are made up almost entirely of people below fifty years of age, with members of the West Indian community being roughly seven to ten years younger per family than the Indians and Pakistanis. Occasionally one encounters an older person, but that is the exception rather than the rule. Older dependants usually bring health problems and a greater demand on the social services. The older people we have met have always been males, and they have always had a command of the English language, which gives rise to the conclusion that they have come over here in order to help the family to settle and integrate as quickly as possible. This appears to apply only to the Indians and Pakistanis, and not to the West Indians.

At the time of writing, the effects of the Commonwealth Immigrants Act have not been felt in Huddersfield, for numbers have risen rapidly rather than shown any sign of abatement. Possibly this is because the need for a work permit, and therefore guarantee of employment, gives male immigrants a feeling of security, and they are thereby encouraged to bring their families. Between 1960 and 1962, single men, or married men bringing perhaps one son, formed the greatest part of the immigrant intake locally. Now we find that we are receiving whole family units in greater numbers, attracted by economic opportunity and a comparatively favourable housing situation.

And it is with the arrival in Huddersfield of whole families that our problem at Spring Grove has become more acute. The efforts we make with our pupils from overseas are directed all the time at their successful absorption into the British social system, although at times we have felt presumptuous in attempting to impose the customs of an industrial and technological environment upon Asiatics from an agrarian society.

The voluntary movement of people between countries has the effect of transforming the host nation into a kaleidoscope of ethnic groups with differing cultures. However small these groups may be, if they are to achieve successful readjustment in new surroundings, efforts must be made by immigrants and hosts to make the business of living together as smooth as possible under the circumstances. Most people would agree that if newcomers to this country wish to live here permanently they must accept not only the rights and benefits of citizenship, but also the duties and responsibilities. We, in our turn, must remember that we as hosts also have responsibilities to our new citizens.

The post-war tendency all over the world has been for the majority of immigrants to be young people. For example, in Australia between 1946 and 1954, three-quarters of the total number of immigrants were aged between fifteen and forty-nine, and approximately one-fifth were children under fifteen years of age. Likewise in this country immigrants tend to be young people or members of family units with young children.

This provides us with two age groups who will need our help both socially and educationally. The adults on the one hand, and the children on the other, will each have differing problems.

For the adults the material benefits we can offer are fairly obvious—a higher standard of living and social security. We must accept the fact, nevertheless, that these alone are not enough. Although many of our new citizens already speak our language, there are many more who do not. Usually the adults, particularly those from less highly-developed Commonwealth countries, have had only limited educational opportunities, and we could make more effort to reach them through whatever methods of communication are available. Where no provisions yet exist, courses at Colleges of Technology and other establishments of further education should be initiated in order to provide facilities for those adult immigrants who have a genuine desire to master their second language. Simple printed language guides could be published, whilst voluntary organizations should be encouraged to give language instruction.

By making the fullest use of the educational aids at its disposal, the receiving country will then have played its part in ensuring that the immigrant obtains a basic knowledge of our language in order to understand what we might term his 'two R's'—his rights and responsibilities.

The lack of means of communication between two ethnic groups can provide the greatest barrier of all to successful integration, but even when the obstacle is overcome, the battle is only half won. Real social integration can truly be achieved only with the support and co-operation of an enlightened public who understand the needs of the immigrants, and who will not be impatient of early teething problems.

CHAPTER III

SOCIAL AND CULTURAL PROBLEMS

When the Indian and Pakistani children in their *shulwars* (pyjama-type trousers), tunics and flowing scarves of colourful silk cross the threshold into our grey school building, they seem to bring an Arabian Nights atmosphere of colour and mystery. They bring, too, experience of a culture so different from our own that their lessons within the classroom must be the least bewildering of their encounters with our way of life.

In the majority of cases the children will not have had experience of an English school building, and the intricacies of stairs, galleries and classrooms must present an overwhelming problem to the small figure as he stands in the large hall gazing, rather lost and bewildered, at his new surroundings. The children's introduction to school follows hard upon their sudden transfer from a simple existence in a sunny Indian or Pakistani village to a terrifying conglomeration of lofty, soot-begrimed buildings, noise, rushing traffic, busy people, blended together with rain, fog, and possibly a rather diluted sun.

To us, our hard-working industrial towns of solid, trustworthy stone represent security and prosperity, but they can only appear as something from a nightmare to children who, in all probability, have had no educational or emotional preparation for their flight to a new home.

From the purely physical point of view, the thin silks of the girls' tunics and trousers appear pitifully inadequate protection against the rigours of a damp, foggy, and ice-cold winter. However, the few minutes spent changing for physical education lessons soon reveal that under the exotic surface, layers of gaily coloured, hand-knitted woollies provide practical evidence of the efforts of Indian and Pakistani families to adapt themselves to the differences in our climate. More recently the majority of immigrant families have shown their awareness of the rigours of our winters by travelling here between August and November, and so acclimatizing themselves for the months of December, January, and February. The following figures of admissions of children from overseas underline the change of pattern as the immigrant community becomes more firmly established.

Year	Total Immigrant Admissions during the Following Months	
	1 September–30 November	1 December–28 February
1959–60	4	4
1960–61	11	10
1961–62	22	16
1962–63	23	16
1963–64	70	24
1964–65	64	21

The Sikh Indian girls, in fact, often adopt the jumpers and skirts, or 'trews', of their English counterparts, quite soon after their arrival, but the Pakistani Muslim girls rarely discard their national clothing and prefer to make concessions to the weather by discreet out-of-sight additions to their wardrobe. The boys of both nations, on the other hand, wear European clothing from the start, often with some style, and find winter comfort in the uniformly popular navy blue duffle-coat.

The Sikh surnames present something of a problem in that, on account of their religion, all the male Sikhs are called 'Singh' and all the females are called 'Kaur'. Even on marriage the lady retains this surname and is referred to as 'Mrs. Kaur'. However, one Indian mother made a great concession by insisting that, not only should her daughter be called Singh, but she herself should be called 'Mrs. Singh' and not 'Mrs. Kaur'. Further confusion arises when several children in the same class bear not only the same surname but the same first name. In one class the arrival of three girls, all called 'Shindo Kaur', caused the teacher to classify them, for her own use, as 'Long-faced Shindo', 'Round-faced Shindo', and 'Belinda', whilst other teachers in similar circumstances have referred to children as 'Gurdeve 1' and 'Gurdeve 2'.

Seldom do the Sikh boys living in Huddersfield area retain their long hair, usually an essential outward sign of their faith.

In fact the occasional ones who do are regarded almost with
curiosity by Sikh children who have been in this country for
some time, and who have forgotten how different was the
appearance of the menfolk in their native Punjab. This was
brought home most strikingly when one of the older boys,
Hardial, removed his gaily coloured turban to take part in
a physical education lesson and all his fellow-Sikhs exclaimed,
'Oh, look, he have long hair!' We still get a great deal of
pleasure, however, from welcoming Rajan's grandfather into
our school in his bejewelled turban and with his flowing grey
beard—truly a majestic patriarch. We were also delighted
when Grandfather Samra, as he is affectionately known, won
his battle with his employers, British Railways, and was
allowed to appear at work wearing both his turban and his
guard's badge of office.

Of course, the clothing and habits of our own English children appear equally strange to the immigrants. In fact their
senses are assailed by a variety of new sensations. The Asian
child must feel himself to be an island, surrounded by a raging
torrent of a sea, formed by new and frightening sounds—of
children chattering in an unknown tongue, of the weird music
of voice and piano, and the boisterous bouncing on wooden
floors in physical education lessons. Even the teacher's voice has
a different timbre and until a feeling of security and affection
can be established, the meaningless and unfamiliar cacophony
of sounds in a bustling Primary school can only intimidate.
It is possibly a little alarming to the newcomer at first to hear
children of his own nationality chatting in a strange tongue
and being understood.

Not only do the ears of these children have to adjust themselves abruptly to a new stimulus, but so also do the hands.
Suddenly they are having to learn to manipulate the tools and
equipment of learning, not only the basic essentials like crayons,
paper, and books, but also the more sophisticated educational
aids, like constructional toys, Wendy houses, jig-saw puzzles,
and craft materials such as plasticine. With older children, the
hands that are often more accustomed to handling a plough
have to be trained to handle a pencil and a ruler. To English
children the school piano is a familiar, entertaining, and com-
forting piece of furniture, but to the immigrant child it has to

be met and, as with the tape-recorder or physical education apparatus, sized up and become familiar, before being accepted.

A large number of our Indian and Pakistani children live near enough to the school not to need school dinners, but for those who do stay for meals, the assault on the palate is yet another battle to be fought in the settling-down process. Religious scruples present a minor problem as far as menu is concerned, for the immigrant children receive the same freedom of choice as do our own children. The Indian Sikh children do not eat beef, because of the sacred position held by the cow, and the Muslims are not able to eat pork. Fortunately an understanding school meals department and a sympathetic kitchen staff have enabled this particular hurdle to be overcome quite simply by providing extra protein vegetables for the children who prefer not to eat meat, and so partly compensate for the lack of meat in their diet.

Knives, forks, and spoons present a challenge at first, until the children become accustomed to them, but the process of adapting is remarkably swift. In one way the children who do not stay to school meals give us more anxiety than those who do. Fortunately in most cases a meal, if only a small one, is waiting for the children when they return home at lunch-time, but all too often, if father is on shift work and sleeping during the day, a meal is not forthcoming. This is particularly likely if mother has not yet come to England and the household is all-male. In fact sometimes the children will spend the lunch-hour walking around the town, for it is not worth while going home; and they often hang around the playground for long periods, after the end of morning school, and then quickly return after being sent away by the teacher on duty. This happens far more regularly with the Pakistani children because, of all our ethnic groups, they are the ones whose mothers are most likely to remain in their native lands, as many of their menfolk are here for only short spells and for purely economic reasons.

Among the more bewildering experiences of the Indian and Pakistani child on his first day in school is his first introduction to the niceties of the English plumbing system, with pedestal seats and flush operation. Many of the children have never used such equipment, relying perhaps in their own villages on the natural facilities offered by the field at the back of the house, or, at the best, on a very primitive closet arrangement.

At first they attempt to stand on the seats of the school toilets in their endeavour to squat on them as they have been accustomed to squatting on the floor. We have found it expedient, therefore, to train the children in the use of the toilets from the very first day, with the help of the older and very tactful Indian and Pakistani children. 'Reminder' lessons on hygiene and toilet habits from time to time, with the teacher drawing water-closets and our method of using them, on the blackboard, are received in a highly good-natured and unself-conscious fashion by the children, who show appreciation of the artistic efforts by saying what 'lovely lavatories' they are. Picture flash cards, too, depicting the 'do's' and 'don'ts' of behaviour in toilet hygiene have proved most effective. This approach, together with the co-operation of a very understanding caretaker and cleaning staff, has kept this kind of problem down to a minimum. Furthermore, working on our principle that these children are the finest second-generation ambassadors, we hope they will be able to train the rest of their families in these basic habits.

In spite of the rigours of the English winter we have always been pleased to find our immigrant children extremely hardy, with an unexpectedly high resistance to coughs, colds, and influenza. They are excellent attenders, with the weekly percentage of attendances never very far short of 100 per cent. They seem to suffer from few of the childish ailments, possibly because they are now immune, having been exposed to them all in rapid succession in their early childhood in their native country.

The only two ailments which give us cause for anxiety are scabies and tuberculosis. The isolated outbreaks of scabies have been dealt with most effectively by the school clinic, and we have been most fortunate in the fact that only very few of our immigrant children have been found to be suffering from active tuberculosis. Understandably, however, English parents are extremely anxious about the possibility of their children contracting the disease, since it is well known that there is a high incidence of the disease among adult Indians, Pakistanis, and West Indians.

To allay these anxieties and to protect immigrant as well as English children, the new arrivals are medically examined by the school doctor as soon as possible after arrival, and the examination includes a tuberculosis skin test, by arrangement with the local health authorities. For this we are indeed grateful, as it not only allows for the immediate treatment of any disease but it also reassures parents and members of staff. Even when medical examinations are provided, the problem is often far from being solved, because of the fear of officialdom, and of possible medical expense, on the part of the immigrants. In a neighbouring town a child was discovered by the school medical officer to be suffering very badly from rickets. When asked to attend the local clinic for medical treatment he did not appear, nor did he return to school again. An intensive house-to-house search yielded no trace of his whereabouts, but he was eventually found by another young compatriot less than twenty minutes after the headmistress had explained that it would be for the benefit of his health, and at no extra cost, for him to attend the clinic. If medical examinations were conducted in this way, at national level, upon all immigrants entering this country, and if settling were dependent upon a clear bill of health, some of the social problems which weigh heavily upon administrators and social workers could be scotched at source. It would also, perhaps, help to alleviate one of the causes of animosity felt by our own countrymen to coloured Commonwealth settlers.

From the educational and administrative point of view, medical examinations tax the school staff to the utmost. The usual form sent home to parents on these occasions requires them to supply information about the dates when their children suffered from various illnesses. For English families this is usually a simple matter, but, when neither parents nor children understand the written word, the completion of these forms can present a formidable task. It is at these times that the teacher's artistic and dramatic abilities are given full rein, drawing bodies covered with various types of spots and demonstrating in a most lifelike manner St. Vitus's dance or whooping cough. And when the forms are eventually returned, the entries penned with such labour and difficulty are often colourful and amusing and not always exactly what was required.

The multiplicity of races being educated within the school walls (at one stage as many as twenty-one different nationalities have been included on the school roll) brings also a multiplicity of religious beliefs with their attendant customs and rituals of behaviour. Morning assembly presents few problems, since at Primary level the teaching of religious doctrine would be out of place. Each week a different class is responsible for conducting the assembly and the children choose the theme for the week and also the music, the hymns, the lesson-readers, and the prayers; and on one day they are responsible for the whole of the service. Children of many nationalities and many faiths, therefore, are joined together in our daily worship, which as well as being as simple as possible allows that although the children may pray together, they each pray to their own God. The non-Christian immigrant children greatly appreciate stories about Jesus, or stories from the Bible in which good triumphs over evil. They understand fully that we are not attempting in any way to inculcate the Christian faith, but that in the same way that we endeavour to understand and tolerate their beliefs, we ask them to learn a little about ours. The Muslims, in fact, hold the figure of Jesus in great reverence as one of the world's great prophets. One older boy did request that, when the rest of the school closed their eyes to pray, he would prefer to keep his eyes open as he liked to see his God.

It is in the realm of social customs and behaviour that differences in religious beliefs make themselves most emphatically felt. The Indian Sikhs from the Punjab are a tolerant people who are prepared to adapt their beliefs more quickly than most immigrants to the English way of life, and apart from their objection to the eating of beef, their religion has remained a private and uncomplicated affair. The Muslims on the other hand insist upon a social code for believers that cuts sharply across accepted patterns of behaviour both in school and out. And it is the older Muslim girls who are most affected.

A major obstacle to their comfortable integration is the fact that their clothing is symbolic of their position in life. The parents of Muslim girls in our school insist that no parts of their bodies should be visible in public except for the face, hands, and feet. During normal day-to-day class activities this presents no problems. In marked contrast the voluminous trousers and tunics which look so enchanting when the girls move about the school, bring nothing but cumbersome complications and entanglements when worn for physical education or netball—in fact, in the latter activity, girls have been known to use their clothing to hide the ball. For a boy to set eyes upon the bare arms or legs of a Muslim girl would bring the direst social consequences, even to the point of ruining her marriage prospects and making her very much a second-class citizen. For this reason only very rarely have the Pakistani girls been persuaded to change into suitable clothing for physical activities. We have always believed it vital to develop their bodies as well as their minds, so some form of physical education is necessary each week.

Swimming too—a compulsory lesson for all our children over nine years of age, unless medically excused—caused much heart-searching until efforts were made, by reorganizing time-tables, to ensure that these girls and boys received instruction separately, and on the strict understanding that no male teacher nor any of the boys should be permitted to enter the swimming baths or its surrounds until the girls were safely away. In this way, East and West came to an amicable solution.

There still remain the more practical difficulties of exotic flowing dresses when viewed in the light of English climatic conditions. Girls who arrive in driving rain or walk through several inches of snow or slush, cannot sit all day in sodden trousers; and we do all we can to promote the wearing of sensible weather-proof clothing. Boys often take to wearing wellington boots, but so far the girls have remained impervious to suggestions on these lines.

Our greatest anxiety occurs during the festival of *Ramzan*, when Muslims fast for one month, allowing no food, water or any substance of any sort to pass their lips between the hours of sunrise and sunset. This takes place in January and February, and in a kindly climate, and where possibly little exertion is required, the children could be expected to cope reasonably well with the situation. In bitterly cold weather, however, many of our Muslim pupils find it almost impossible to make the necessary effort at their studies, and to combat the effects of the cold weather. In fact, on several occasions, our teachers have had to deal with children fainting in the classroom from lack of nourishment. Although they are permitted to eat before sunrise, if they or their parents happen to oversleep they may have to wait until evening before eating again, making twenty-four hours in all without food. Although very young children are not expected to fast, it often happens that parents who do not cook for themselves, will not bother to cook for the young ones. Probably our first knowledge of Ramzan was when several Muslims asked permission to be excused taking part in a swimming lesson because of the fact that no water should touch their lips. They were granted permission and resumed swimming immediately the celebration was over; but this was the oddest excuse ever heard for 'not going to the baths'.

However, the physical aspects of the differing religious beliefs are overshadowed, from the long-term point of view, by the emotional stresses which inevitably arise when the requirements of any society encourage children to adopt a different attitude to each other from that which would normally prevail in their native country.

In Muslim society the woman holds a backstage position, and even in Huddersfield, purdah is observed as far as is humanly possible. Pakistani menfolk usually do the family marketing, take washing to the launderette, and deal with all the contacts outside the home, while the women can go no further than garden or back yard for their fresh air and exercise. If the women do go out, it is common practice for them to walk a few paces in the rear of the men.

In contrast to the position of their mothers, the Muslim girls enjoy more freedom of movement and of privilege during school hours. They are treated as English children are, without discrimination between the sexes. They are taught, with English children, a feeling of independence, and the little social courtesies which we consider so essential to the pleasant running of society, such as allowing girls to pass through a door first, or helping them to carry things. Above all both sexes are conditioned to mixing freely in all activities and to be outward-looking in everything they do.

For this reason, the older girls in particular must be only too painfully aware of the conflicts between their position at school and place at home. Although more and more Indian girls,

c

when they leave school, take up employment in the textile trade, where their nimble fingers can be put to the best advantage, it is still the custom of the Pakistani girl to revert to the normal Muslim practice of purdah the very moment she attains school-leaving age. She merely remains at home, continuing the preparation for marriage which was begun in early childhood, when her parents arranged her marriage. This has been the custom for many centuries and cannot be eradicated overnight.

Betrothal celebrations among children of both Indian and Pakistani families are commonplace, yet all the time, television, cinemas, and literature are proclaiming the Western ways of life, leading to even greater tensions among young people of the immigrant community. Over the years, the more integrated with our way of life the young people become, the more they will estrange themselves from their elders and the culture which was their birthright. Boys, too, have similar difficulties, for the free-and-easy attitude here to the social mixing of the sexes can encourage adolescents to misinterpret and go too far. This lack of perspective, contingent upon unawareness of real, rather than artificial, circumstances, has been evident in some secondary modern schools. Fortunately the incidents have been isolated in themselves and sympathetic handling by the Heads and staffs concerned has enabled matters to be smoothed out quickly. A useful factor in such circumstances is the awe in which these children hold their parents and the mere mention of reporting the affair to their fathers has an immediate and desired effect. However, we must continue to be hypersensitive to all forms of tension and take the greatest of care not to aggravate them.

Initially, our contact with the parents caused us to think that they were being co-operative, as the children frequently mentioned the help given them on particular points; and occasionally parents would ask for the teacher's explanation of details which were proving troublesome. But, as the immigrant communities increased, and the rate of admission became more rapid, we noticed that parental help and interest virtually disappeared. Apart from the initial encounter with father, uncle, or English-speaking friend of the family, when children were first admitted, we seldom met them again. However, recent months have seen some improvement in the situation, and it was heart-warming to see a number of women dressed in saris at a Christmas Carol Service not long ago.

The possible reasons for the lack of a working relationship between school and parents are numerous and largely conjectural. Obviously the language barrier may discourage parents from visiting the school, although on Open Days we have always undertaken to provide an interpreter. Our recent efforts to reach them more efficaciously by sending home letters in Punjabi and Urdu have met with more success. Open Day in the summer of 1965 saw many more Indian or Pakistani fathers, or family friends. This leaves us with the impression that typewritten letters in English were pushed to one side and neglected, possibly because they represented officialdom, which they regard with some suspicion. Yet we believe that letters in English can emphasize to parents their obligation to learn our language. Male members of the household who work difficult shifts or night work may well find it impossible to come to talk to teachers; but, having stressed to all parents that the school is always open to visitors, we feel that the situation has improved considerably. On talking with the parents we have been most impressed lately with the fervent interest in the progress of their children, particularly the boys, for whom a good British education provides a badge of success. It has been evident that even with letters home in Punjabi and Urdu there can sometimes be a breakdown in communications, as when both children and parents alike thought that our jumble sale, for which we had whipped up feverish enthusiasm, was a sort of religious festival. It must be recorded that, in spite of this, the 'jungle sale' was well attended and much enjoyed.

It has been most noticeable that the children who do receive help and encouragement at home make far more rapid progress than their fellows and, because this is the most fruitful way of breaking down the first-generation barrier, this is encouraged as much as possible. Mustasum, who was a complete beginner as an eleven-year-old pupil at our school in February 1964, was, in January 1965, ready for transfer to the Grammar stream of a Secondary school. This was due partly to his innate ability, partly due to his early work at Spring Grove, and, in no small measure, to a willing and enthusiastic uncle whose work with the boy at home has proved invaluable. In the same way, Rajan's successful selection from Grammar school in 1964 owed something to the encouragement of Grandfather S., and similarly another grandfather friend is helping his granddaughter Shabnam with the complexities of the English language.

These two gentlemen, although having many qualities in common, are dissimilar in appearance. Grandfather S. is a tall, military man, of commanding figure and majestic carriage, complete with waxed moustache and typical Sikh beard. He now leads the Sikh community in Huddersfield, and after serving for over twenty years as an officer in the Indian Army, he organizes his family with almost military precision. Although a graduate and obviously experienced in undertaking responsibility and leadership, he has accepted his dramatic change of position to that of a British Railways' guard, with the philosophical resignation one associates with the East.

Grandfather Q. is short of stature with a dignified bearing and handsome features, including a short pointed beard. All who meet him are impressed by his quiet dignity and old-world courtesy. He loves children, and is often to be seen walking to school with English as well as Pakistani children clutching his hands. He usually wears a dark overcoat and astrakhan hat, but in deference to our wet weather he sometimes dons a plastic 'mac' and the Yorkshireman's traditional flat cap, much to our delight. Whilst several Indian and Pakistani friends have been regular visitors for a number of years, these two grandfathers have given us infinite pleasure, and their dignity, wisdom, and consistent friendliness and helpfulness have been much appreciated by the staff.

Social customs regarding the position of womenfolk in Pakistan and India have militated against our seeing very much of the mothers of our immigrant children, and to this factor must be added an innate shyness, and an almost universal inability to speak our language. But even the women are becoming more venturesome, and the past two years have seen a slight but definite growth in the number of Indian and Pakistani mothers who come to see us. One bolder individual came one day to ask if her ten-year-old son could leave his class to hold her baby while she went to do some shopping. On being told very gently by the head of the Special English Department that this was not possible, she countered, 'You hold him, then!'

Generally speaking, it is possible that the strata of society our children come from do not yield the type of adults who could act as leaders, either in organizing a general approach to school, or in providing a bridge between their own cultures. Possibly it is traditional in the home countries for parents not to take an active part in school affairs. Possibly, too, school may be rather forbidding to adults who have received little or no education themselves. The persistent use of the native tongue in the home, to which the mother is largely confined, does not help her to learn English and therefore to make contacts outside. The women who do go out can usually manage to confine their shopping expeditions to the many Indian and Pakistani grocers and butchers near their homes, ensuring that they rarely need to use English. At the hospital or at the doctor's surgery they can always take one of their English-speaking children to interpret. Unfortunately, their need for interpreters also occasionally means that children are kept away from school to help mother shop at the open market held each Monday afternoon. Whenever we meet parents we stress the importance of the family's speaking English at home as much as possible in order not to nullify the work we are doing at school.

The West Indians, the other large group of immigrants in the school, present fewer practical social problems, for they are generally well clothed, clean and tidy, and their health and attendance are good. However, their different attitude to family relationships and their easy-going approach to life is very noticeable in the emotional reactions of the children.

A striking feature is the position of the mother in the home, for throughout it appears that she is often the dominant factor in the family, and is almost always a wage-earner and provider. We have found that where parents have shown sufficient interest in the progress of their children to visit the school, they have tended to give their support individually rather than together, although in the majority of cases it has been the mother who has called to discuss the problems and future prospects of her child. This probably stems from a social background in which concubinage and unmarried parents are commonplace, and in which seasonal work for the menfolk, and subsequent periods of poverty, lead to a large measure of economic dependence upon the mother. This in its turn has led to the establishment of unofficial 'day nurseries' in which a woman might have as many as fifteen children in her care, often in abysmally inadequate and unsafe premises. Fires caused by oil-heaters have been known to occur in such premises, with tragic results.

Where both parents are working it often arises that the children feel unwanted and uncared-for. They are not encouraged to join in the conversation of their elders, nor to feel that they are an integral part of a family unit. When placed in large classes it is small wonder that these factors, added to the already present language difficulties, cause them to feel subjugated. It is only when they take part in small group tutorials that their linguistic abilities are allowed full scope.

Yet another social phenomenon is created by the arrival in England of West Indian children who have come to join their parents, having spent most of their early childhood in the care of their maternal grandmother. They show signs of having been spoiled and kept as babies for far too long. Their emotional ability to cope with new surroundings is much affected by this, and by the fact that their parents are almost strangers to them. This is true particularly in the case of the father, who sometimes aggravates matters by a tendency to violence if the child does not make what he considers to be reasonable progress. We have on more than one occasion heard a West Indian father say 'I'se gonna give him a beating.'

Education of immigrant children does not consist merely of the imparting of the English language and the academic skills. If properly and conscientiously carried out it involves a deep understanding of the social and cultural backgrounds from which the children come, and a constant effort to help them adjust socially and emotionally to the demands that are likely to be made upon them.

CHAPTER IV

THE DEVELOPMENT OF THE EXPERIMENT

The language teaching scheme grew logically to meet the needs of constantly changing circumstances, eventually producing an English language school, within a school. At first, when the numbers of children needing attention were small, part-time English tutorial classes were sufficient to help the non-English-speaking child. Three years later a full-time class was felt to be more practical and productive educationally, eventually leading to a number of graded full-time Special English classes, under one school roof. All non-English-speaking children from five to fifteen years old were directed here, and were integrated, when proficient, into the Junior Department at Spring Grove, or into normal classes in schools near their own homes. In this way the academic progress of the English children was not impeded by the increasing numbers of non-English-speaking immigrant children, and, at the same time, the immigrant children were receiving the maximum educational benefits that we could provide.

In 1958 Spring Grove was an ordinary Primary school, with two Infants' classes and four Junior classes, serving the town-centre area population. The school itself had recently been re-organized from a 'through' school, with boys and girls aged from five to fifteen years, to a Primary school, and understandably there were still traces of the atmosphere which usually surrounds a school where older children have been catered for and have made their mark.

There were 181 children on the school roll, of whom a quarter were not English. As often happens in declining areas, immigrants had been attracted by the cheapness of the property, and perhaps by the comparatively large size of the houses, making for easy and lucrative subletting. This latter consideration became more important with the advent of West Indians, Indians, and Pakistanis.

It was already becoming apparent that with the increase in enrolment of non-English-speaking children, not only in the Spring Grove area, but throughout the town, it would be necessary to take more positive action to help both the children and the teaching staff. Consequently a survey was made in September 1958 by the Huddersfield Education Authority, in order to determine the extent of the need. A questionnaire was sent to the heads of all the schools in Huddersfield, both Primary and Secondary, which, in addition to asking for the normal details of age, sex, and nationality, also asked the length of time each pupil had been in this country, and the standards reached in their written and spoken English.

The returns, when received, listed thirty-two children of immigrants, of whom nineteen were Indian, one was Pakistani, and twelve were Europeans, comprising Poles, Yugoslavs, one Hungarian, and one Italian. Of these children eighteen were of Infant and Junior age, the majority of them already attending Spring Grove, and fourteen of Secondary age who were attending Secondary schools in the borough. In fact, roughly 80 per cent of those children needing help with English already lived in the area served by our school. Since we had extra teaching space available and were centrally situated, it was decided that we should become the centre for a new scheme of special tutorial classes for non-English-speaking children. We realized that because of the signs of depreciating property, the increase in the numbers of non-European immigrant families in the immediate vicinity of the school, and the start of group settlements, the next few years would see a vast change in the type of children who would pass through the school.

A Swedish woman was appointed to take charge of the Special English tutorial work, and this provided us with our first asset—a teacher who had already had to learn English as a second language. She was, therefore, better equipped than most people to understand many of the difficulties which beset a foreigner learning English for the first time. To offset this, her spoken English was good but not perfect, though happily it improved.

It was decided that the children should leave their ordinary classes at our own and other schools at regular times during the week for their Special English lessons, and the timetable was so arranged that Secondary schoolchildren and Primary school-children were taught at different times, in view of the necessary difference in approach. This naturally called for a high degree of co-operation between head teachers, class teachers, and the Special English tutor, to decide which lessons on the normal timetable could most easily be foregone by the children. Wherever possible arrangements were made to ensure that the children of Secondary age received a maximum number of English lessons from their own school and from Spring Grove. This was largely because we considered that in view of the short time left to these children before they became workers, their need for formal English tuition was more urgent.

Most of the children who entered the scheme at its inception had already spent some months, or even a year or more, in an English school, and therefore in the early stages we had few, if any, complete beginners. Our efforts were directed mainly to improving the standard already reached, concentrating particu-larly on written work and reading. As well as written grammar exercises, the English teacher used a variety of methods to im-prove conversational ability and reading. Toy shops, word games, modelling, 'Look and Say' matching cards, as well as many home-made visual aids, were extremely valuable. When they were not receiving special tuition the immigrant children returned to normal classes. If there were only a few with poor English in any class an imaginative teacher could absorb them without great difficulty, and by dint of a little extra attention, and the perpetual efforts at communication by their classmates, they could not help but improve their English.

This immediate absorption into classes is of course the ideal way to achieve integration, both linguistic and social, and it can work extremely well while immigrant numbers are small, and as long as neither group is in any way retarded by the situation.

Inevitably the tutorial English work in the early days was handicapped by the lack of suitable books and materials, and by the fact that it was new and experimental. We had to use existing English grammar and reading books which were far from suited to our specialized task, for most books used even in the younger classes of an English school rightly assume a fluent ability in the spoken word, with automatic comprehension, for instance, of changes of tense. Improvization and much experimentation with home-made visual aids was to be the pattern throughout the early years, taxing the ingenuity of the staff to the utmost. Another difficulty was lack of continuity, since, on many occasions, the Special English teacher had temporarily to suspend the tutorial classes in order to substitute for sick members of staff in the Primary department.

This tutorial work on a part-time basis, with children leaving their normal classes at set times during the week to participate, continued until 1961. During the period of its operation it had been most rewarding for us to be able to return a large number of children of differing nationalities permanently to their normal curriculum. Progress could be measured; for instance, between 1958 and 1959, Jarneil—a fourteen-year-old Indian boy—increased his reading age from 7·9 to 10·3 years, while Bogdana—a thirteen-year-old Yugoslav girl—improved the percentage in her English language examination results from 50 per cent to 66 per cent. Asghar—a thirteen-year-old Pakistani boy—likewise achieved in problem arithmetic an age rating of 13·2 years in 1959, comparing very favourably with his age rating of 10·8 in 1958.

Regular reports from class teachers at our own and other schools left us in no doubt as to the success of the scheme. This success was marked not only in the academic improvement in the work of the children but also in the type of warm relationship that was building up between the children in our Special English scheme, and the staff and other children in the school.

In 1961 the general problem was to become more acute, for by now more children were arriving from India, with no English at all, and when joining a class in sixes and sevens proved to be a much more difficult proposition for the teacher— almost an embarrassment, since the tremendous amount of attention needed by these children had of necessity to be sapped from that given to the rest of the class. This was particularly difficult in a school like Spring Grove, where there is only one class for each age group, with four ability groups in each class. For instance, one class contains thirty-nine children with reading ages ranging from 15·2 years down to 6·4 years—the top and bottom children being Ukrainian and Polish respectively.

Class teachers rose nobly to the new situation, but in such conditions the most brilliant teacher would be taxed to the utmost, and at that time, with growing numbers of non-English-speaking immigrants, the position was becoming untenable. Teachers obtained some relief while these children were attending their Special English classes, but for the rest of the time it was becoming impossible to absorb them into the class unit at all constructively, for most of what the teacher was saying in subjects like geography, nature study, or history, was well beyond their comprehension. They felt bewildered and out of their depth, and the teachers inevitably felt frustrated, for if they spent all the time that they would wish in helping the immigrant children and making them feel secure, they would be sacrificing part of the timetable, already tightly scheduled, to meet the demands of the present system of selection tests used by the local education authority.

Stage two in the evolution of the Spring Grove project was reached when, after much careful thought at Spring Grove and discussion with the Education Department, it was decided that in order to relieve the classes in the Junior school, all non-English-speaking children of Primary school age should be gathered into one full-time class. Gradually they were returned to their schools as their ability in English improved.

By this time we were beginning to receive news of the first successes achieved by children who had passed through our initial tutorial classes and had returned to their ordinary schools. Manjit and Mohan, both at Secondary Modern schools, had earned prizes awarded to children who had made the most progress during the year. Also Balhar, another ex-pupil, was transferred to the Grammar stream at another Secondary school, under the Local Authority's 'Late Developer' scheme.

We had been most reluctant to 'segregate in order to integrate', but it became increasingly apparent as time went on that the new method was paying rich dividends in terms of successful transfers back to normal school classes.

Since the establishment of the original class of sixteen children with one teacher, our Special English department has grown vigorously. It now contains seven classes and over 130 children with six full-time and some part-time teachers; instead of having one small offshoot class within a school, we are now virtually two schools within one.

By the summer of 1961 we were noticing a change in the population pattern of the area we serve. Where European immigrants had been in the majority in the early stages, we realized that these families were gradually moving away from the town centre as they achieved economic stability, and their places were being taken by large numbers of Indian, Pakistani, and West Indian families. This led gradually to a greater pro-portion of coloured children to white.

Nevertheless, when white families did move away, it was most gratifying to us that parents, both European and native British, often asked that their children be permitted to stay on at Spring Grove School—this often in spite of long travelling distances in poor weather.

During the early months of 1961 the problem grew apace. More and more children were arriving from India and Pakistan, with as many as twenty-two new arrivals in ten days. Since an increasing proportion of children were of Secondary age, it was decided, after consultation with the Local Education Authority, that all children with a language problem, no matter what their age, should be enrolled at Spring Grove. They could then be transferred to our Primary department or to Primary or Secondary schools near their homes when their ability in English was adequate.

Since there were no satisfactory tests for us to use for deciding when a child was ready to leave our Special English classes, the only yardstick we could employ, and still do employ, was a personal and individual assessment by the headmaster and the class teacher. This system has worked very well and each child's case has been given most careful consideration before transfer, taking both educational and psychological factors into account.

By September 1961 it so happened that most of the children of Secondary age were between eleven and thirteen years old, and even after some months with us, when they had begun to achieve some degree of spoken and written fluency, their ability tended to approximate to that of a ten-year-old child because of their late start in the use of the English language. As the teachers engaged on this work in the Special English department were all experienced Primary school teachers, it was felt that their more 'Junior school' approach would be both appropriate and effective, and it was soon obvious that they were able to cope satisfactorily with the demands placed on them by these children.

Experience was teaching us that in a Secondary Modern school, particularly one without a remedial group, the non-English-speaking child often became 'lost' and insecure, especially since each teacher met him in only a few lessons each week, and he could easily be overlooked and his interests not catered for.

With the arrival of a second full-time teacher for the Special English department in September 1961, it was possible to divide the now much-swollen Special English class into two. It was decided that a 'transfer class' should be established to provide a very necessary bridge from the rather rarefied atmosphere of the Special English group to the more exacting demands of a normal English class.

Fifteen children were allocated to this class, and it was agreed that English should be the only language used within the classroom, not only between teacher and children, but among the children themselves. The children readily accepted this decision, and made it a matter of personal pride to comply. They were told that any persistent offender would be 'demoted' to the beginners' class; this would have involved a great loss of 'face', and on only one occasion did it have to be enforced. After persistently speaking in Punjabi, Lakvhir was told by the teacher of the transfer class that he must report to Class 1. He left the classroom shamefacedly, and after walking round the school several times he returned to his own class and announced that the other teacher would not have him. He felt that his honour had been retrieved and never spoke Punjabi again in the classroom.

As well as being highly practical, the setting up of the 'transfer' class gave a psychological fillip to the children, because those who formed it had the constant incentive of being transferred to normal classes, and likewise those of the lower class were anxious to prove themselves ready to progress to the transfer class as soon as possible.

Meanwhile the rapid increase in the admissions of immigrant

children swelled the ranks of the lower class still further, and by Easter of 1962 we were able to establish a third full-time class, thus separating complete beginners from those with a little knowledge of English.

In the spring of 1963 a new milestone was reached when our population of coloured immigrant children in school exceeded that of the white children by 136 to 135, and the number of the Special English department reached a new 'high' of eighty-five. Our present figures are revealing. Out of a total roll of 320 children, the coloured immigrant children now number 173 to 147 white children, whilst there are 131 originally non-English-speaking children in the Special English department. A final analysis shows that out of 320 children on roll, 211 are of immigrant origin, the vast majority of whom were born over-seas.

CHAPTER V

THE AIMS AND APPLICATION OF THE EXPERIMENT

At the time of writing our Special English department is divided into seven classes, accommodated in rooms of various sizes throughout the school. The seventh class was set up when pressure of numbers was so great that we were obliged to convert our newly equipped four-booth language laboratory into a classroom for older beginners.

There are three beginners' classes, with children selected very roughly according to age and sometimes size. The five- to seven-year-olds form one group, and the seven- to eleven-year-olds the second, and finally we have the eleven- to fifteen-year-olds, who provide a beginners' class of Secondary age. Occasionally, if an eight-year-old is very small, he joins the Infants' class, or possibly a very tall ten-year-old will feel happier in the 'teenage' beginners' class. As their English improves, the two younger groups pass through the progress classes to the final 'transfer' class, while the older children, who have far less time at their disposal, reach the transfer class after passing through only one progress class.

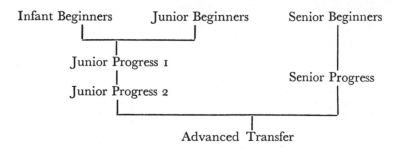

It might be assumed that once a beginners' class is established, the work of the teacher, if not easy, would at least be straightforward, since all the children enrolled in these classes have in common the need to learn the English language. But there are three factors which affect the manner in which the teachers may present their work and the methods they may use.

First, it is probable, particularly in the case of children over seven years of age, that many of them have already been to school in their own country. They have acquired the basic skills in reading and writing in their own language, and some ability in dealing with number, often to a high degree. They also have a knowledge of class discipline and general social behaviour. At the same time others have never been to school in their lives, have never held a pencil or crayon and find the school environment completely alien. Inevitably those who do have the basic skills are more receptive educationally, while the others need to be taught to hold a pencil with the teacher's hand firmly grasping their own, and how to count up to five.

This has been the case with numbers of Indian children who come knowing nothing but how to perform labouring tasks on the farm. An eleven-year-old boy admitted that when the local law in the town where he lived decreed that education should be compulsory, he was smuggled away to the country to live on his uncle's farm and so avoid going to school.

Nationality also has considerable bearing upon the initial teaching of English. It so happens that present trends in immigrant population patterns in Huddersfield predetermine that the majority of the children admitted for English teaching are Indian and Pakistani, although, in the past, Central Europeans have been very much in evidence. We do have occasional Italians and Spaniards, however, and it is inevitable that European children will learn more quickly. To begin with they do at least have an alphabet in common with us, leading to much more rapidly acquired skill in reading and writing the English language. The Indians and Pakistanis, on the other hand, have to learn a completely new set of symbols, and often a new direction of handwriting from left to right.

Also, in common with most English children, our European pupils have experienced the type of educational climate at home which ensures that a little pre-school training has been forthcoming.

With Infants, the problem of language learning is not nearly so great as with older children, since they have almost certainly not learned to read and write in their own language, and are starting from the beginning in the same way as any English child. Often, if they pick up conversational English with a degree of speed, they can be transferred to an ordinary Infants' class and take their chance quite successfully with English children. One or two terms in the Infant beginners' class do, however, give them not only a much-needed basic knowledge of oral English, but a chance to adjust themselves to a new way of life before they take their places in normal school routine.

In 1961, for an experimental period, we decided to place six immigrant infants, with no English, directly into the ordinary infants' reception class, in order to test the theory that language is not a barrier at the start of a child's education. Success was very limited, in spite of the attempts of the teacher to give individual attention where possible. They were slow at first to join in class activities, being more inclined to favour individual efforts, such as crayoning and plasticine, which enabled them to withdraw into themselves. They were handicapped not only by their inability to understand English but also by their lack of pre-school training in such things as number recognition, counting, building games, and constructive play. Consequently their progress in both conversational English and in their class-work was very slow compared with that of the other children in the class, although after the initial setbacks, they eventually showed some slow but quite definite signs of advancement.

With one, two, or three immigrant Infants placed in an English class, success would be likely, but with higher numbers the teacher cannot give the necessary extra attention. Our present Special English Infants class has twenty-five children on roll, which would make it a practical impossibility to attempt immediate integration at Infant level.

Sometimes, in addition to being able to cope successfully with school subjects in their own language, the older children have learned English in India and Pakistan. The method by which they are taught, however, ensures that, although they may be able to read quite fluently, they understand very little of what they are reading. Furthermore, they are often unable to converse at all in English. They have obviously learned by some mechanical method, usually involving the learning by heart of fables, proverbs, and moral sayings.

Abdul, a fourteen-year-old Pakistani boy, interspersed pages of arithmetic with high-minded admonitions to his teacher, beautifully illuminated with designs of roses and trellised leaves, such as 'A bad workman blames his tools', and, more dramatically, 'The fruits of rashness is repentance'. The same boy, in order to impress the teacher with his ability to write fluent English, wrote from memory one of Aesop's fables; but when questioned about individual words and phrases, showed that he did not understand them.

Another grave difficulty in planning a scheme of work, and in teaching it successfully in the classroom, is the irregularity of times of admission. This is a problem we have so far been unable to solve. Enrolments of immigrant children at Spring Grove are not restricted to the beginning of term, not even to the beginning of the month, but children arrive in ones and twos, week by week, and even day by day. The teachers then have to attempt to absorb the new children as they arrive, endeavouring to provide them with a feeling of security and a warmth of welcome, giving them extra attention, while at the same time keeping existing and more advanced residents happy.

One possible solution would be to exclude these newcomers until a prearranged admission day, possibly at the beginning of a term and then again at half-term, allowing the teachers to have at least six weeks of uninterrupted work. This would no doubt bring legal complications, since it would hardly be fair to allow one group of children to stay away from school quite legally, while English parents are being prosecuted for the non-attendance of their children.

Another suggestion is that all newcomers should be retained in a 'buffer' class until the Special English classes are ready to receive the next intake, with the time being occupied by activities designed to adapt them to a new school routine. Further consideration could well be given to the idea that the person in charge of such a class should be an Urdu-speaking teacher, this being the most common mother tongue in this department. An immediate disadvantage would be noticed if some of the non-English-speaking pupils were not Urdu-speakers. However, certain advantages would obtain for there would be available a teacher to whom the children could talk and whom they would understand, and he or she would be able to provide them with the very necessary feeling of security in the early days. Furthermore, his or her help would be invaluable in early social training, both in general school behaviour and in hygiene. Finally, the attempt could be made to provide some continuity in education for those children who had received some education in their own country, until such a time as they should move into the Special English department.

Educationally, the eleven- to fifteen-year-olds bring a special problem of their own, in that, particularly with the older children, we are working against time to equip them for the outside world. Many of them have the prospect of only one year at school before having to start work, and it is not easy in such a short time to teach them to speak, read, and write English to any degree of fluency. To offset this handicap, these children have a tremendous desire to work hard, and an ability to apply themselves, which is partly inherent, partly helped by any previous educational training they may have had, and partly instilled into them at home by families whose greatest wish is that they should reap the utmost benefit from a 'British education'.

Whenever possible we try to persuade under-equipped fifteen-year-old children to stay on at school a little longer, for not only is there a chance that their English will benefit by a few extra weeks in the classroom but also, when leaving at mid-term, they will not have to face the great and increasing competition from the normal end-of-term Secondary school-leavers. Occasionally a father has insisted that his son leave school in order to supplement the family income but most prefer their children to reap the maximum benefit from the educational facilities available.

As the children pass through the Special English department, the more advanced classes endeavour gradually to introduce a scheme of work which is similar in design, if not in depth, to that found in a normal English Primary class. In this way, as they pass through each grade, they are coming closer to what they may find when they leave the department.

Our two Infants' classes and four Junior classes are prepared to receive children when they are transferred, and are able to carry on where the specialist teacher left off in integrating the immigrant children. The actual time of removal depends very much on the progress of the individual child. Many pass right through the department before being proficient enough to leave, while others make such rapid progress that they are able to move out to the Primary department, without going through all the grades of Special English classes.

When they do leave the department, however, the Primary-age children usually go to a class one year below their own age group, in order to acclimatize them to the different atmosphere of an English classroom, moving up when they are able to cope. Secondary school-age children likewise spend a term in our final Junior class before leaving for Secondary schools near their homes. Our arrangements are always flexible, both in transferring children, and in moving them between Special English classes, and we usually find that by the end of the Primary course, those children of Primary age who have been integrated have found their normal level of attainment. Also worthy of note is the fact that our assessments have been reasonably accurate and no child has had to be returned to the department.

This close interrelation between the Primary department and the Special English department at Spring Grove is vital to the success of our scheme; it ensures firstly that our immigrant children learn English as quickly as possible, and secondly that English children in no way suffer in the initial teething pains of integration. In fact they all gain eventually from the infinite richness of growing up in a multiracial school.

CHAPTER VI
METHODS OF APPROACH

Throughout the Special English department we use the Direct Method of teaching our language; that is, as well as being the subject taught, English is also the medium through which it is taught. We do this first because it is the quickest and most effective way of teaching a second language to children and, secondly, for the very good reason that with classes composed of differing nationalities, unless the teacher is a veritable polyglot, it is the only practical method.

When the children first arrive in school, the essential task for the teacher is to make them feel welcome and secure in their new surroundings. It must be remembered that most of them have been transplanted almost overnight from conditions dramatically different from those in which they suddenly find themselves. So many leave primitive, sunny villages in India and Pakistan, with little or no traffic except bullock carts, and a school which often consists of only a patch of ground under a shady tree, with both teacher and pupil sitting cross-legged.

To them, the school building, in its vast greyness, and the general hubbub and activity of a busy Primary school must seem overwhelming, almost terrifying, even without the strangeness of the English climate, the town, the traffic, the soot, and the dingy mill chimneys.

For the first few days in school the children invariably look frightened, withdrawn, almost haunted, and where with English-speaking children one could comfort and reassure with words, with these children one can only smile and hold their hands, and with a firm, gentle voice, say things which although not understood, will, by tone, give a sense of security. The average English child usually takes a few weeks to settle down comfortably into a new school routine; how much more difficult it must be for the children who have so many more new psychological and physical experiences to contend with. Also the physical reassurance we can give them is of twofold value, in providing an emotional bridge between home and school.

During their early weeks with us, they learn by sight, touch, and sound to connect objects and items of furniture in the classrooms with the names of these objects. They learn to answer the questions: 'What is your name?' 'How old are you?' Also, by example, the teacher will introduce simple orders. For instance, 'Sit down—open your desk—take out your pencil'. Soon the flow of words used by the teacher will become meaningful, and with pictures, more objects and toys, and various activities in the classroom and about the school, the sphere of comprehension of the children will have widened considerably.

In the following weeks and months, more and more English structures are built up, helped by word games, stories, action dialogues, with constant repetition and correction, relating everything as far as possible to everyday life. The home and family relationships, are something we all have in common, and which always provide a valuable approach in conversational English. Likewise transport is a lively topic, since the density of the traffic here makes a dramatic impression on the children.

They attempt to tell the teacher their daily news, and any occurrence, however trivial, can be turned to good advantage as a subject for conversation—going to the market with mother, a visit to the cinema or even a shoelace broken when changing for a games lesson. When twelve-year-old Darshan broke her arm it proved to be a blessing in disguise, for her visits to the infirmary for X-rays and examinations by the doctor, and the final removal of the plaster, provided a lively topic for discussion for almost a month. As well as being an occasion for teaching all the vocabulary connected with doctors, nurses, and the hospital, it provided an opportunity to give practice on how to use all the medical services.

The natural sequence of learning a language is simple and logical. The first requirement is that the child should understand the flow of words he hears. From the first understanding, initial efforts at speaking follow naturally, and soon it is possible to introduce some simple reading, provided that it is connected with vocabulary already familiar to the child. Finally, when he has the feeling of security engendered by being able to express himself fairly fluently in his new language, he will attempt, at first haltingly, but eventually freely, to compose simple sentences in writing.

The fact that the children are with us all day and every day, from nine until four, is at once an advantage and the source of a problem. Because their education is completely in our hands, we are able to plan a scheme of work to build up their knowledge of English gradually and systematically, and we can adapt it where necessary to suit the needs of individual children. We transfer children between Special English classes as soon as they are ready, so our schemes are of necessity very flexible.

On the other hand, a day lasting from nine until four is very long, and obviously if the children are to be kept interested, happy, and alert, the timetable cannot consist of one long English lesson. Consequently, they undertake a wide variety of activities during the school day. Although large slices of the timetable are devoted to conversational English and the mastering of English grammatical structure, there are lessons in art, craft, needlework, physical education, swimming and games, as well as the obvious essential work in number, reading, writing, and other basic skills. Not only do these lessons enable the children to exercise their newly developing powers both physically and creatively, but they also provide admirable opportunities for teaching them the language of each subject—in physical education such words and phrases as 'handstand', 'climb the rope', 'jump over the box', 'lift the mat', and 'batting' and 'bowling', whilst in needlework they become acquainted with the names of objects such as needles, thimbles, and thread and such techniques as hemming and casting on.

We have come to learn that all school routine becomes a series of lessons, and can be turned to good account; school meals, changing for physical education, milk, moving about the school, road safety, morning assembly, medicals, hygiene, and toilet-training—these are all talking points. A great deal of vocabulary and colloquial English is absorbed by the children during these activities, and since many of them are daily, they have the hidden value of constituting repetitive exercises.

Our approach within the classroom naturally varies according to the age and ability of the children. In the lowest class the curriculum is very similar to that in any ordinary Infants' class, for the Infant method lends itself extremely well to the teaching of English as a foreign language to this particular age group. In all the beginners' classes we have often found a box of small toys and other objects to be of great value, not only in teaching items of vocabulary, but also in the use of prepositions and adjectives of colour, size, and shape. None of our Special English classes is without a box of miscellaneous objects, which will perhaps include such things as cups, spoons, knives, forks, toy animals, flowers and trees, toy motor-cars and buses, doll's house furniture, buttons, needles, pins, and thread. The teacher can ask questions about any object from the box—where it is (on the table, under the desk, in the box, on top of the cupboard), what shape it is, what colour it is, how many wheels or legs it has. Later, it is possible to play games with the toys, such as Kim's Game, or even Twenty Questions, and finally the children can buy or sell them in the classroom toy-shop.

Colourful wall pictures, charts, and flannel-graphs are very useful, and teachers spend many hours making their own visual aids in the form of models, pictures (either cut out of magazines or drawn), and flash cards, to illustrate verbs of action, vocabulary, or any structure or situation they wish to explain. In the same way picture-books, postcards, and even such things as travel folders, can be put to very good use.

A large toy clock with movable hands is indispensable, and the children soon learn to tell the time in English, which gives them a great feeling of confidence. This confidence is essential as our demands on time are vastly different from anything they have previously encountered. Once they reach an industrial area, they need to make a quite definite and conscious effort to readjust themselves to the rush, bustle, and increased activity and, understandably, awareness of time plays a much greater part in their lives.

Naturally our approach to the Secondary school-age children is more adult, but basically the order in which structures are introduced, and the methods by which they are taught, are the same for all age groups. Each teacher adapts the syllabus to suit the appetites and interests of the age group with which he is dealing.

Once the children have even a limited vocabulary it is possible to introduce subjects like nature study, geography, social studies, and even science in a very simple form. We have lessons about coal mines, railways, air travel, wool, cotton, and the life cycle of the silk-worm. In the spring each class has a large number of tadpoles, collected from the lake in a local wood. The children grow their own hyacinths and daffodils in order to compete in our annual bulb show. Butterflies and moths are always a popular study, while the children are fascinated to compare farming methods in their own country with the methods used here. With books, pictures, films, models, and other visual aids, these topics are an extension of more formal English lessons, and introduce the children not only to fresh areas of vocabulary, but often also teach them much about their new surroundings and way of life.

There is an infinite variety of classroom activities to which teachers can resort in their efforts to present English to the children and to encourage them to speak it spontaneously and without shyness. Apart from classroom shops, Wendy houses, and sand play, the Puppet Theatre is very popular among the younger children; they compose for it their own often very dramatic dialogues. At a more advanced level, the transfer class have performed short plays on occasions, although the impact of 'Cinderella' was somewhat marred by the refusal of the heroine to dance with Prince Charming, or even to hold his hand, since such action was strongly against her moral and religious principles.

Stories are always tremendously popular, as are poems and rhymes, the repetition of which is valuable for exercising pronunciation and intonation. Word games, crossword puzzles, and Bingo, together with 'Ludo' and 'Happy Families', all played entirely in English, provide linguistic practice in a number of ways, while sugaring the pill a little. We use films and film-strips on many topics, to good effect, and, of course, the tape-recorder is a great asset.

We have perpetually to 'pre-teach' in order to teach anything at all. For example, in pattern painting, we first have to teach the words paint, colour, water, and brush. Then we have to explain where a pattern is found—on wall-paper, dresses, and carpets; then wall-paper, dresses, and carpets need explaining, and so on *ad infinitum*.

The mechanical side of arithmetic usually comes very easily to Indian and Pakistani children, but they are gravely handicapped at the beginning by their lack of knowledge of English. Where possible lessons in arithmetic consist partly of some practical activities, such as weighing, measuring, and capacity, so that each child has some concept of the language of number. Likewise it is most useful to do conversational work involving the English monetary system, as well as the ordinary mechanical exercises. Oral mental arithmetic conducted as a class activity provides a foundation for the eventual ability to cope with written problems, for which the children must also be able to read.

In the middle-progress classes it is possible to compile a time-table of work approximating more closely to the syllabus of an ordinary Primary school though still in a much simplified form, but English is still the pivot upon which all other activities revolve. The children learn the concept of future and past tenses in various ways, and continue building upon the foundation laid in the beginners' classes. At this stage too, more attention is paid to reading and writing.

By the time they reach the transfer class the children are speaking relatively fluently, and the time is spent largely on con-solidation and in constant practice in the use of English in as many situations as possible. At various times the classrooms have been a café, a shop, a police station, a doctor's surgery, and a post office, in which the children have been able to exercise their abilities in a really practical way.

In the post office the children deposit counterfeited money in post office savings books they have made themselves; they make parcels, write, post, and sort letters, cash pensions, and buy television licences, taking it in turns to be customers and counter clerks. We have received considerable help from the General Post Office, who have been most generous in providing sample telegram forms, customs declarations, and even two internal telephones, so that the children are able to learn how to make and receive telephone calls. One delighted visitor was told by a very busy young official in the Spring Grove 'post office' that he was sorting letters into 'budgie-holes'. The installation of the two dry-battery telephones in a classroom has proved to be a most valuable aid for the development of free expression, and both instruments are constantly in use throughout the day. All the children become skilled in using them and boys and girls from the department are trained to answer the school telephone in the headmaster's room, so increasing their sense of responsibility. One of the many rewards provided by our work with these children came when Mindi, a ten-year-old Indian boy, after less than twelve months in this country, used a public telephone to ring his teacher and inquire about her health when she was absent from school through illness.

The setting-up of the police station was a natural follow-up to a visit made by the class to the Huddersfield Borough Police headquarters, and the project reached a fitting climax when a police officer visited the class and gave an illustrated talk on Crime Prevention. This also serves to underline the excellent co-operation we receive from the local police force, especially their Juvenile Liaison Department and the Road Safety Officers.

Occasionally the classroom takes on a medical atmosphere and whilst one of the children acts as the doctor, the 'patients' must be able to describe accurately the symptoms of their particular ailments. In fact, there has often been strong competition between the children to concoct illnesses which would stump the doctor. However, he has always coped successfully with broken bones, stomach-ache, and even a patient who alleged that he had been bitten by a snake in nearby Greenhead Park. Only once was he nonplussed, and that was when a case of a broken leg already a week old, insisted that he had telephoned three times and that the doctor had refused to come. These activities have also helped in explaining the need for school medical examinations, and it must be confessed that all the teachers have found it highly taxing to explain to children with little English what mumps, measles, and whooping-cough are. At times when medical examinations are taking place it is not unusual to see blackboards covered with bodies in turn covered with spots, or having other disabilities, with the teacher at the same time coughing her heart out to give more lifelike demonstrations.

As well as being, in reality, yet further English lessons, these activities have unlimited social value. Many of the social services, particularly the Post Office and the medical services, must have experienced great difficulty when confronted with a customer or a patient who could speak no English, and who could neither explain his difficulty, nor understand any advice or instructions given to him. Many half-days of school work are lost by our older children who are needed to act as interpreters for relatives visiting the doctor or the hospital. During the smallpox epidemic a few years ago, an auxiliary nurse said that it was a blessing that English-speaking children had been available to help cope with non-English-speaking adults in their families.

Visits outside school are a regular occurrence; perhaps to the fire station, or to the 'launderette', to the railway station or a careers exhibition, or simply a walk to the nearby park or the woods. As well as being educational, these outings have considerable value in social training. The children learn to move about the town in a quiet, dignified manner, and we feel that it is a vitally important part of our social integration work that the general public meet these children, both individually and collectively, on such expeditions, and realize that they are ordinary children receiving the same type of education, of the same standard, as other children. We hope that society will accept its very necessary part in helping the children to achieve complete integration.

Lessons in physical education and games are much enjoyed by the immigrant children, but somewhat unexpectedly we find that the Indians and Pakistanis are far from agile, and lack confidence in physical activity. They tend to be heavy and flat-footed in their movements, particularly the girls, who normally run in a clumsy and ungainly fashion. This is possibly due to the fact that in their own countries they often wear moccasin-type sandals with no arch support, or they wear no shoes at all. They do, however, show considerable grace in their hand movements, suggesting that hand dancing would give them pleasure. We thought at first that these girls were perhaps a little lazy, but we have learned by experience that their social customs and culture have militated against physical activity. These remarks apply, not only to the general movements and muscular co-ordination of both boys and girls but to their performance on apparatus. It is immediately apparent that they have had little, if any, experience of apparatus work—in fact, if they have received any physical education at all in their native lands it has been of the very old-fashioned 'drill' variety in fixed-standing positions. Because of a slightly wider than normal age range in the classes, the lessons have to be planned with great care, in order to provide activities and skills which will benefit the weakest and extend the most courageous, whilst encouraging each child to play his part both as an individual and as member of a team.

Music lessons too, can be somewhat discouraging since there is a wide difference between our own tonal system and the oriental one. When our Indian and Pakistani children first hear English singing, or English music of any sort, they are usually convulsed with laughter. However, they soon become familiar with the sounds and begin to participate a little in our musical activities. This ability to adjust ear and voice is more rapid and effective in the very young children, who are quickly able to sing nursery rhymes quite tunefully, but with older children their own musical patterns have had longer to become deeply ingrained, and their enjoyment is more passive, though in common with other young people of today they show an immediate and spontaneous liking for the Beatles.

So far we have outlined only the methods used in our Special English department, but the success of the scheme is very dependent upon the excellent follow-up work done by the teachers in the main school, who with infinite patience continue the work of integrating the children to whom we have given the basic essentials of the English language. They are helped by the fact that, as with the Special English department, the timetable is flexible and can be adjusted at the discretion of each teacher to suit the appetite and the needs of the class.

We are also coming round to the view that because of the changing character and background of a large proportion of the children in the main Primary school, our history and geography lessons will have to be adjusted more realistically. At present the history syllabus consists of 90 per cent English history—not an appropriate balance for children of whom large numbers come from India, Pakistan, the West Indies, and Central Europe, and to whom it would be of advantage to learn something of their own history and geography. To this end we would make more use of the Discovery and Project system, at the same time introducing more general science into the curriculum.

Friends in the educational world and visitors to the school have often suggested that full-time Special English education must impose an impossible strain on both children and teachers. However, we can only say most emphatically that there is never any indication of strain in any of our children. On the contrary their relaxed and happy attitude to school and to their teachers, coupled with a purposeful desire to work hard, is one of the vital ingredients in the success of the scheme. This would not be possible without a balanced academic diet and an imaginative and varied approach to the task. The greatest demand upon the teacher in this type of education is that he or she should be very flexible in his or her methods, and should be highly sensitive to danger signals of flagging interest and restlessness. Admittedly this can be taxing, but the relationship between teachers and children is one of such affection and happiness that the rewards far outweigh the hard work that is demanded.

CHAPTER VII

VISUAL AIDS AND
EDUCATIONAL EQUIPMENT

The direct method of teaching a foreign language requires the maximum amount of child participation, and there is always an insatiable demand for colourful pictures, models, and 'handling' materials of every description, in order to give a visual and tactile impression of the new situations, words, and objects which children are encountering throughout the school day. Of necessity, in the early weeks, oral work is far more important than any attempts at reading and writing, for comprehension and early efforts to speak require the constant provocation and encouragement provided by visual aids of infinite variety.

Our early work relied almost entirely on home-made apparatus, and the teachers' oldest and firmest friends, the blackboard, chalk, and duster. The success of their use depended entirely upon the teacher's dexterity and imagination in depicting a situation, and with children who could not have differences explained to them in any other way, accuracy in expression was essential. He or she might simply have to explain differences in adjectives—big, small, tall, short—or, at the other end of the scale, a whole town might be called for, complete with cinema, traffic roundabout, and zebra-crossings.

Pictures on the classroom walls, too, are a tremendous help in teaching the English language. Pictures telling a story, pictures describing the weather and the seasons, pictures showing shops, hospitals, railway stations, or farms—each one helps to add to vocabulary and grammatical structures. They can stimulate the interest of the children, and when the vocabulary becomes familiar they can provide the confidence so vital to progress. The children can return to the pictures, or likewise to drawings or models they have made themselves, for a feeling of security. It is desirable that each picture must be not only large, colourful, and exciting, and with a minimum of written expression, but must present as many different actions as possible. We have found that, among other material, the Longmans, Green and Co. General Service Wall Pictures satisfy these requirements admirably.

At present there is an ever-increasing amount of visual material being made available commercially, but this has not always been the case. Initially the making of apparatus by hand made great inroads on the individual teacher's ingenuity, skill, and time, as well as drawing heavily upon consumable stock. Matching cards, with pictures and numbers, were in evidence very early in the scheme, perhaps illustrating verbs, colours, and adjectives. Those for a specific purpose had to be designed and constructed by the teacher, who alone knew the requirements of her class. Such items included weather charts, with words and illustrations, days-of-the-week charts, materials for practising the use of our monetary system, and equipment for teaching how to tell the time. Invariably there was also to be found a home-made chart for teaching tenses or prepositions, in different colours and with movable strips containing words which the children could change to suit the time or the situation. For example a monitor's chart might read: 'Yesterday Jaswinder gave out the milk, today Jit gives out the milk, tomorrow Mussarat will give out the milk.'

We have probably manufactured more 'flash cards' than any other school of comparable size, for we have found the technique one of our greatest assets, and its uses are legion. Now that felt-tipped pens are readily available, reliable and easy-to-read flash cards are quickly made and are a reasonably lasting product. They are usually large pieces of card with either words or pictures on them in bold print or line drawings, which are held up by the teacher at the front of the class, and can be seen clearly by each child, wherever he or she is sitting. In the teaching of reading they are an aid to word recognition, either in single words or, eventually, in whole sentences. These sentences may give orders or ask questions to which the children can respond in a variety of ways. Pictorially they help the acquisition of vocabulary; for example, a few firm, simple lines on white card can produce the response, 'The fat man is running', or 'The boat is upside down'. All lessons involve a period of revision as the teacher moves from the known to the unknown, and, here again, flash cards can help, providing the security of a familiar situation.

Obviously toys and scale models of such things as cars, buses, and dolls' houses have a great value in teaching vocabulary, as well as actual articles found in the home or in school, but the children gain great pleasure and satisfaction from making their own models. Not only the finished product—perhaps a village or a farm complete with houses, trees, and inhabitants—but also the actual manufacture, from cartons, newspaper, and many other raw materials, help to increase vocabulary and knowledge of English grammatical structures. All the teacher's explanations and orders have to be in English, and the children learn at the same time as keeping their hands occupied in a creative way. The duplicator is in constant use, perhaps providing individual working sheets illustrating items of vocabulary such as clothing, forms of transport, or animals, or simple but appealing diagrams depicting adverbs or prepositions. We are indeed indebted to our liaison with Strathearn School in Montreal (described in a later chapter), for, as well as receiving copies of books used, we were delighted to have many copies of duplicated material used in the school as a teaching aid.

The direct method of language teaching requires that each new structure and sentence pattern should be presented as attractively as possible, and this involves a large variety of presentations. Sets of posters or charts have always been in demand to supplement the very necessary oral drills. We have made extensive use of such posters and charts provided by commercial firms, and those donated by local travel agents. Unfortunately, such paper visual aids have a habit of curling up or getting torn, and soon become unattractive, particularly if they are constantly handled by a number of teachers and children.

Early material sent to us from Sydney, Australia, included a set of pictures entitled 'Language Picture Series No. 1', to provide supplementary visual situations which would be readily available for teachers. The pictures illustrated various activities in the home and garden, and also contained clocks to set the time of day of each picture and to assist in the teaching of telling the time. As the teacher would be able to handle these sets easily, they could be shown to the class as a whole, or demonstrated to an individual child. For a long time the nearest similarity to the Australian idea which we could use was the 'flannel-graph' system, whereby an environmental situation, such as 'the kitchen' or 'the bathroom', could be constructed with flannel models, arranged and rearranged to suit the needs of the children. Members of staff have sometimes designed their own, but good use has been made of the interchangeable back-cloths and different subjects produced by Visigraph in their 'Safety in the Home', 'The Farm', and 'Road Safety' flannel-graphs. More recently an excellent series has been marketed, and has provided us with a wide variety of situations and a comprehensive vocabulary, using a plastic material instead of flannel. This is the range of Cellograph visual aids, produced by Philip and Tacey.

Our experiences have proved to us beyond doubt that all material should be accurate, clear, and meaningful. It must be changed regularly and occasionally reintroduced for revision. By adhering to these methods the children will learn to use their eyes as well as their ears and mouths, when learning to speak a new language.

We have stressed elsewhere that our method of teaching the non-English-speaking child has been based on a definite order of approach, that of understanding, speaking, reading, and writing. Consequently, it is desirable that all reading and writing of new words should take place after they have been learned orally. Only recently has there been produced a suitably graded course for the teaching of English to Asian children, and our early work was noteworthy for its experimentation and adaptation of methods of introducing English structures and vocabulary in the most natural order.

At first, we attempted to adapt reading-books used in ordinary Primary schools, but with little success. First reading-books for English children are able to make use of a variety of tenses and prepositions, for all English children comprehend the idea of past, present, and future, and words such as over, under, through, and between. It is useless for non-English-speaking children to learn to read sentences using the past tense until this stage of English grammatical structure has been introduced at the logical moment in the scheme of work. Later we tried, and found useful, books designed for the slower readers. Amongst the first ones used at Spring Grove were Gertrude Keir's *Adventures in Reading* and *Adventures in Writing*, together with the appropriate pupils' work books.

In 1961 we were introduced to a new series called *New Nation English* by Bruce Pattison. The course is designed for five- to seven-year-old children entering school with no knowledge of English. Although it was specifically intended to meet the needs of African children, and all the pictures, situations, and vocabulary are clearly African, it did provide us with valuable material at a time when we were establishing our first full-time class of completely non-English-speaking children. The series consists of a pre-reader, containing pictures and picture-stories for oral work only. This leads on to first and second reading-books, and the set is accompanied by teachers' work books, which help teachers not only in the use of the textbooks but in the general methods of language teaching. It still plays a useful part in our work.

In order to obtain and maintain each child's interest in the written word, we have also found useful such books as *Let's Learn to Read* by J. Taylor and T. Inglesby (London, Blackie, 1960), *Racing to Read* by A. E. Tansley and R. H. Nicholls (London, Arnold, 1962), and *Sound Sense* by A. E. Tansley (London, Arnold, 1960). The *Gay Colour Books* (Arnold) are particularly valuable for our purpose because of their simplicity and their repetitive quality.

In 1962 we added to our English scheme by making full use throughout the department of the series by Ronald Ridout entitled *International English*, published by Macmillan. The five graded books combine reading with writing practice, introducing English grammatical structures by means of simple sketches, substitution exercises, and exercises in free construction of sentences. Although these books were, and still are, a great help to us, we were still searching for a course which was suited to our particular children. By 1963 almost all our non-English-speaking immigrant children were Indians and Pakistanis, and for this reason we welcomed the arrival on the educational scene of the *Peak* series for Asian children, produced at the Special Centre in Nairobi, and published by the Oxford University Press. The Special Centre is part of the Ministry of Education in Kenya, under the directorship of Charles

O'Hagan, and was set up in 1957 to study and experiment with the teaching of English in Primary schools. In addition to evolving a new method, it also undertakes the training of teachers.

Because the *Peak* series has been specially designed for Asian children it reflects the interests of our children at Spring Grove. It uses Indian names and the pictures have an Indian flavour. In the early books 'Mother' and 'Father' are portrayed in the Indian clothes so familiar to our children, and not in Western dress. The series begins with a colour picture-book, or pre-reader, followed by a 'link reader', after which there are progressive graded readers, accompanied by associated work books, covering a three-year programme. Accompanying each section is a comprehensive teacher's book, which sets out in detail the vocabulary and structures to be taught, and the order in which they should be introduced. It also includes help on the teaching and exercise of pronunciation, stress, and intonation.

Now that our Special English teaching is organized on progressive lines from beginners' classes, through progress classes to advanced transfer, we are able to follow a constructive and logical course by using the *Peak* series as a basis for all our work. Under the flexible arrangement whereby various children move forward from one class to another at different times during the term or year, it is now possible, indeed essential, for the teacher to have an accurate progress report of each child, and the advantage of a course used consistently throughout the department is that the receiving teacher can continue smoothly where the previous teacher left off.

In order to supplement the reading material, and in order to provide interesting and appealing work for our children, we have found the *Oxford Colour Reading Books*, by Carver and Stowasser, very valuable. The coloured pictures and simple vocabulary are full of action, and appeal to the humour and sense of adventure of the children. Some of the pictures bear labels to help word-recognition, and the words are repeated in various contexts. The stories and situations invariably provide an immediate conversational stimulus, while the word puzzles and games are an added interest.

Similarly attractive are the *Ladybird* books, particularly the *Keyword Reading Scheme*. As the name suggests, some words,

which are used more than others, are the 'keywords' of our
tongue, research having shown that 300 of these words make up
three-quarters of our children's reading vocabulary. We have,
therefore, found the controlled and progressively graded vocabulary, with its repetition and carry-over from one book to
another, extremely helpful when teaching a new language. The
series, which is attractively illustrated, is also used by the
younger children in the main school, and so once again continuity is maintained when children from the Special English
department are transferred.

The teaching staff have been indebted to books on method
such as *English Through Actions* by H. E. Palmer and D. Palmer
(London, 1959), and *The Teaching of Structural Words and
Sentence Patterns* by A. S. Hornby (London, 1962). Also useful
for teachers' general reading have been E. V. Gatenby's
Direct Method English Course (London, 1953), and *Living English
Structure* by W. Stannard Allen (London, 1959).

The *Oxford Colour Reading Books* previously mentioned have
been particularly valuable in aiding the progress of another
special group in our school. When West Indian children
reach 'reading-readiness' they have often done so after a
slow start, either through general unpreparedness when they
are admitted to school at five years old, or because they have
joined us in the Junior department after a scanty education in
the West Indies. They, therefore, require reading material
which is simple yet interesting at their own age level, and the
'Colour Reading Books' provide all that is needed to appeal to
the high-spirited, colour-loving instincts of these children.

In our attempts to satisfy their needs we have also experi-
mented with books specially written with a cultural background
of the West Indies, including stories of the legendary Anancy.
The *Caribbean Readers* by Collins give us an insight into the life
and folk-lore of the islands which constitute the West Indies.
J. D. Bentley's *Words Together* and *English Language Practice for
the West Indies,* together with a series for teaching English to
Primary classes by Gabriel Wong, have been most helpful in
ironing out the remarkable differences between Standard and
Creole English. Cassidy's scholarly work, *Jamaica Talk,* provides a much fuller and fascinating study of Jamaican grammar, and makes delightful reading as well as revealing the

difficulties West Indians encounter when obliged to live in a society where their folk-speech is not understood. Finally, we found that *My Mother who fathered me*, by Edith Clarke, enabled us to learn something about the social organization of the West Indies, and her study of the attitudes and relationships amongst the families of three selected communities in Jamaica gave us a vivid picture of those customs which place so much responsibility on the mother.

Another type of visual aid valuable in teaching non-English-speaking children is the film or film-strip. One difficulty we have encountered is one that many teachers will have met, namely the shortage of a suitably equipped room which is readily available. Most old 'town-centre' schools suffer from overcrowding and the ever-increasing demands on classroom space, and although we have been fortunate in having a room 'blacked-out' for the use of visual aids, and all the equipment for showing films and film-strips, the room has been in constant use as a classroom. Whilst in an ordinary school it is often a simple matter for classes to exchange classrooms, the nature of our classes at Spring Grove makes this more difficult. A second obstacle is the lack of vocabulary and understanding of the spoken word by the immigrant children in the early stages. In consequence many films lose their impact and their subsequent value; in fact they become merely an excuse for watching moving pictures. This is not to say that films do not have a part to play in the education of these children, but it is obvious that far greater discrimination must be shown by the teacher when selecting material. Topic appeal is particularly important, and simplicity essential.

In general a film-strip has far greater potential than a film, for with this medium there is always the opportunity to stop and explain, and enlarge upon a particular feature.

All material must be selected to arouse interest and to stimulate the development of language, and our experience has taught us to bear certain facts in mind when choosing films. They should be reasonably short, lasting about ten minutes, and the subject matter should be within the environmental experience of the children. Usually they are interested in people, animals, and activities that go on in the world around them, and the film can therefore be used as a basis for story and conversation periods. The teacher must ensure that the films are well made, up-to-date, accurate in detail, and, where possible, in colour.

Showing a film is no easy task for the teacher, for a great deal of thought and time must go into the preparation of the children to receive the film, and into the very necessary follow-up work. The more frequently films are used, the less likely the children are to regard them as a special occasion, and more likely to regard them as an aid to learning. Most films are now accompanied by teaching notes, which in many cases contain a word-by-word copy of the spoken commentary, enabling the teacher to digest it beforehand and prepare his presentation with it in mind. He must be fully familiar with the working of the projection equipment, but most local authorities now give regular instruction in its use.

We are most fortunate in Huddersfield in having an excellent visual aid department in the Education Offices, who organize regular training courses, as well as assisting in the making of films. The department provides an extensive library of films and film-strips which are well indexed and catalogued for loan purposes. The officers are further responsible for the loan and maintenance of film projectors, film-strip projectors, epidiascopes, language laboratories, radios, record-players, and tape-recorders, as well as the maintenance of equipment owned by schools themselves. Such services, of course, greatly facilitate the work of the individual teacher who conscientiously wishes to make full use of all available teaching aids.

As well as from our own authority's film library, we have often selected films from the Educational Foundation for Visual Aids Catalogue and hired them from the Foundation Film Library in Surrey, where we have always received excellent service.

In the New Year of 1962 the Huddersfield Education Committee decided to purchase some form of language teaching aid and, after discussion between the interested linguists, it was decided that small units of different types of language laboratories should be established in four separate centres in the town. Because of the increasing importance of the second-language work being undertaken at Spring Grove it was decided that a language laboratory unit should be installed in the school.

Whilst it was agreed that a language teaching machine would provide a much-needed innovation in the field of teaching foreign languages to our own children, so that they might attain conversational fluency in the new language as quickly as possible, we were not convinced as to whether it would prove successful with children who could not have explained, in their native tongue, what was required of them when using the machine. However, we hoped to give the machine a thorough trial before passing judgement on it.

Prior to the installation of a permanent unit, we decided to gauge the reactions of our children to a new mechanical teaching aid, and we arranged for a demonstration of the American R.C.A. Mobile Language Laboratory to take place with a selected group of Indian and Pakistani children of varying abilities. Whilst it was obvious that this particular machine would not satisfy our needs, our children quickly adapted themselves to using a mechanical aid and they responded readily to a tape and set of visual images, specially designed for the occasion by a Leeds University colleague.

The spring term of 1963 brought with it the installation of our own language laboratory and a combination of hopes and frustrations. As Spring Grove is a very old school and is a two-storey building with its classrooms grouped round a centrally situated and much-used hall, the question of satisfactorily housing the unit had to be carefully considered. It was finally agreed to house it in a room at the rear of the school and on a lower level than any other room, affectionately known as 'the dungeon'. This position meant that it was furthest from the everyday work of the school and so would provide the quietest atmosphere possible—an absolute essential when planning any work of this nature.

The unit installed at Spring Grove was the first one placed on the market by the Education Foundation for Visual Aids, and the control console, from which the teacher could operate control of the pupils' units, used a Ferrograph deck. This console consisted of a record and playback unit and a master control and was so placed that the teacher could see all the pupils at work. The four-seater pupil's unit had Birmingham Sound Reproduction tape-recorders and a headphone set with a microphone attachment. In each of the pupil's units the controls were reduced to an absolute minimum and the pupils were separated from each other by the hinged lids of the unit. All four units were joined together laterally and, when not in use, the lids provided a table-top working surface.

The largest single obstacle throughout our work in this field has been the complete lack of commercial twin-track tapes specially produced for the teaching of English as a Second Language. Our first efforts at producing such tape and visual material proved to be a very lengthy task, as two members of staff spent approximately fifteen hours preparing a tape which took eight minutes to play. The pictures had to be designed and drawn to match the specially constructed phrases, using simple structures, and the breaks in the tape had to be accurately timed to allow for each child's repetition. We visited the language laboratories at Leeds University and at Chorley Grammar School in order to gain further knowledge of this new work, and joined the National Audio-Visual Language Association in order to share experiences. However, our early efforts were impeded by the constant increase in the number of non-English-speaking children and the shortage of teaching staff.

From our experiences in this very new field of language work we were able to draw the following conclusions. We felt that, first, the children would need careful training in the use of the machinery and in understanding the commands they would hear. They would further need adequate preparation for the structure to be taught, involving elementary drill patterns, and as wide a knowledge of the vocabulary to be used as possible. A most important and vital feature was that the material would have to be carefully selected from familiar situations within the children's environment, and presented in immediately usable sentences. To achieve any degree of success the dialogues would have to be as realistic as possible, with the inclusion of a wide range of sound effects. We realized, too, that the pupils would have to be encouraged in dramatic work—and they would be expected to extend the exchanges of the language laboratory to other situations in their normal classroom activities.

Unfortunately, the efforts of all concerned in our language laboratory work were severely handicapped by several factors. Having only four student booths meant that when a teacher was engaged on work in the language laboratory an extra member of staff was required to cater for the needs of the rest of the class. As our classes are grouped according to ability it would have been difficult to double-up classes. Furthermore, an increasing number of mechanical failures with the machines, and the lack of a local mechanic who was *au fait* with our type of equipment, meant that there was always a time lag when repairs were needed. These early mechanical snags were common to all types of machine at the start and not merely to the equipment we were using. The sound reproduction was not of the highest quality and some outside interference was noticeable. Finally, the increasing numbers of non-English-speaking children entering the school and the need for more teaching space meant that the language laboratory room had to be used full-time as a classroom, with the four booths being used simply as extra desks. Consequently, all language laboratory work, apart from some Primary drill patterns, was discontinued, but we were nevertheless able to learn a number of lessons from our chequered experiments.

Certain basic essentials must be fulfilled before work of this nature can be successful. The room chosen to house the language laboratory must be made as sound-proof as possible, and, if not, a sound-proof booth must be made available where tapes can be made. A good extra tape-recorder is required, with suitable power sockets, in each classroom, so that preparation, repetition, and follow-up work can be carried out during ordinary lesson-time. Also very necessary is a good-quality microphone which is capable of picking up sounds from a distance of up to ten feet, and deadening any sound outside this radius. The minimum number of booths for economical running would appear to be sixteen, thus allowing other larger class units to operate on a half-class basis. Above all, schools preparing to launch into the language laboratory method of language teaching should recognize that it is a very strenuous and time-absorbing medium, and any teacher so engaged could profitably be allowed time, encouragement, and expenses for training. Similarly training colleges would be well advised to include such training in their curriculum. Also, because it is so time-absorbing, it is essential that adequate substitute staff are available during the preparation of tapes and actual language laboratory classes. Above all, commercially produced tapes designed for the teaching of English as a Second Language would substantially curtail the disproportionate amount of time needed if teaching staff made the recordings themselves.

Apart from the more complicated language laboratory, the ordinary tape-recorder, used with imagination in the classroom, provides excellent opportunities for language learning in a variety of ways. We have used it for dramatic work, for oral drills of grammatical structures, for essential practice—pronunciation and intonation—and for help with group reading. Our B.B.C. 'Sarah and Joseph' tapes, discussed in a later chapter, as well as exercising oral drills, also provide a basis for story-time. From the teacher's point of view, the capturing of spontaneous outbursts of English is rewarding as well as recording progress.

We have used the tape-recorder, too, with our West Indian tutorial groups to help with pronunciation and intonation problems, and with French teaching in the Junior school, using methods similar to those in the Special English department.

Finally, from a practical point of view, the tape-recorder should be of the highest quality, with a good microphone, since distorted, woolly speech reproduction is useless in language teaching. The controls should be simple enough to be operated by children as well as teachers, and light enough in weight to be carried easily from one classroom to another. We know from our own experience just how productive the carefully controlled use of visual aids of every description can be. By perpetual experimentation at the domestic level the way has been prepared for manufacturing companies to produce, as quickly as possible, colourful and exciting materials which will attract the children and help their powers of retention. More charts, books, apparatus, tapes, and film materials are urgently needed, in order that more time can be devoted to essential teaching, and less to lengthy hand-preparation of visual aids.

Apart from the teaching of English as a Second Language, great progress has been made in recent years in all forms of language teaching. In many cases the accepted, though somewhat out-dated, methods are being replaced by the new audio-visual approach and other modern techniques. However, the pendulum must not be allowed to swing too far. Each method must be carefully considered and an appropriate, logical place allocated in schemes of work to the old and the new. Oral drills, for instance, have just as important a part to play as the more sophisticated audio-visual teaching aids. A delicately balanced combination of all tried methods will yield the most fruitful results.

CHAPTER VIII

TESTING AND ASSESSMENT

One besetting difficulty which taxes us considerably in our efforts to educate children who speak no English, and who come from widely differing social and cultural backgrounds, is that of their testing and assessment. To be able to evaluate, with justice, a child's educational potential, his intelligence, and his achievements according to the standard of intellectual climate to which he has been exposed, is essential. It is necessary, first of all, upon entry to school so that he may be placed in a suitable class, and so that his teacher can judge the best approach to his problems. Secondly, it is needed at intervals as a guide to the measure of progress he has achieved; and lastly, when he leaves one school for another, or goes to work, an accurate picture of his capabilities is of the utmost value.

Under normal conditions English children can have their progress assessed by the careful use of standardized tests, which compare each child's performance with an attainment 'norm'. Not only do these provide a fairly accurate comparison of a child's ability with that of any other child either in the same school or elsewhere, but they also act as a check upon the teacher's personal assessments based upon his or her observations of a child's work throughout the year. Furthermore, if the tests reveal a lowering of performance, or a particular weakness, the teacher can take steps to remedy them.

Unfortunately, however, the majority of the tests in current use presuppose a knowledge of the English language, both spoken and written, and cannot be used to assess the abilities of non-English-speaking children. Nor can intelligence tests provide a genuine measurement of the intelligence of children who do not speak our language, and who come from cultural environments very different from our own.

Consequently we are left with only one yardstick in reviewing the progress of our immigrant children during their time at school—the teacher's personal assessment of each individual child. This involves regular comparison of one stage with an earlier one, of one child with another of similar age and known similar abilities. It involves, too, judging not only the standard of improvement in speech, vocabulary, comprehension, and the ability to write expressively in English, but also how the child has adapted itself emotionally and socially to the vastly different pattern established by new environmental conditions.

We notice, as the weeks go by, not only the mental adjustment and educational progress of the children, but also perceptible physical changes, marked by improved co-ordination and the lessening of strain that a feeling of security brings. All of these things are quickly registered by the teacher and noted briefly on the individual record cards which are used throughout the school, and which follow each child when he moves from one class to another or out to another school.

Because the children come from such varying educational backgrounds, however, and because their social and psychological adjustment is so important, we have found it a most useful practice for the teacher to write a much more comprehensive and detailed report on each immigrant child for the benefit of the receiving teacher, to augment the information on the ordinary record card. Often the views of more than one teacher are needed to give a composite picture, and the resultant assessment provides a valuable foundation upon which the new teacher can build.

Each report records the child's date of birth, address, sex, and religion together with the date of admission and the extent of the child's knowledge of English on admission. A comprehensive assessment then follows under the following headings: English (which is divided into Understanding, Oral Abilities, Written Abilities, and Reading Age); Number (Mental, Mechanical, and Problems); Physical Education; and finally a general report in which any noteworthy interests or peculiarities are recorded.

These reports are of particular importance when older children leave us to go to local Secondary schools. In a Primary school the class teacher has contact with the children in his or her class for almost all the week, and therefore has ample opportunity for observing and judging the attainments and particular difficulties of each child. With the arrangement of timetables and allocation of staff in Secondary schools, on the other hand, the teachers of the various academic subjects, such as the sciences, history, or geography, may see each child for only a short time each week, and may well find it difficult to decide if a child's progress is being impeded by his lack of the appropriate English vocabulary, or by general low ability.

In many schools teachers are required to make a forecast of the work they plan to do at the beginning of each week, and submit it to the headmaster. We have found it a more useful practice at Spring Grove for each member of staff to keep a record book, in which he or she writes, at the end of each week, a very full and descriptive account of all the work undertaken during the week, and the record of progress made by individual children and differing groups of children within the class. These are handed in to the headmaster on request, and they enable the teacher to look back and compare standards of assimilation and progress from week to week, and from term to term.

The value of these records is appreciated throughout the school, but particularly in the Special English department, for they provide the headmaster and the head of the Special English department with a systematic and comprehensive account of the progress of the children, and the picture presented, combined with the personal assessment of the teachers, facilitates decisions as to when each child is ready to be transferred to another class or to leave the department.

These methods of personal assessment based on the teacher's observation and professional judgement have worked successfully, and headmasters of schools to which our children have been transferred have often said how much they appreciated having a reasonably accurate picture of the abilities of the children they were to receive.

But for children newly arrived from a Commonwealth country, speaking not one word of our language, we have absolutely no means at all of finding out the level of their intelligence, or their academic potential. There are no culture-free tests that we can apply and the situation is further aggravated by discrepancies between the real age of some of the children, and the age that is given on their passports.

As a general principle, we allot children to beginners' classes roughly according to age, and sometimes according to size if the passport is obviously inaccurate. We may discover that a child who has been shy to the point of speechlessness for the first few weeks has actually learned a little English in India, and could with benefit be placed in a slightly more advanced class. Eventually the children are successfully placed in a class to suit their abilities, but occasionally valuable time is wasted, and a child has the unsettling experience of being uprooted from one class to another after only two or three weeks.

In 1961 the Educational Psychologist for Huddersfield became interested in the testing of children who could not speak English. A group of children who were newly arrived in England were chosen as subjects, and an initial experimental attempt to grade them was carried out.

In order to avoid any means of assessment which involved knowledge of English, the tests used were the non-verbal Ravens Coloured Progressive Matrices, which involve the matching and selection of coloured shapes and designs, and the Goodenough 'Draw a Man' intelligence test. Although a normal I.Q. distribution was not expected, it was discovered that there was an almost uniformly low score at or below the fifth percentile on the Ravens test, and an I.Q. of below seventy on the Goodenough test; this seemed to imply educational subnormality and suggested that further investigation was necessary.

It appeared that the accuracy of these tests was in question for a number of possible reasons. In many cases children were unaccustomed to using pencils and therefore to drawing; or because of complete lack of experience they were unable to comprehend the type of simple problems posed by the Ravens tests. Also the fact that many were from a poor area, both socially and economically, undoubtedly contributed to a lower all-round intelligence showing.

It was interesting to observe the comments of two authorities on the application of the Goodenough 'Draw a Man' test to children of similar backgrounds to those tested at Spring Grove. On the testing of 2,500 Indian children from Mewar in 1947, Shrimali noted that 'schoolchildren in Mewar are considerably retarded', and suggested that the points awarded for clothing needed revision. He also made the very relevant comment, which will be understood by all teachers, that 'the drawing is seriously affected by the mood of the children'.[1]

Another psychologist, Anathnath Datta, investigated in 1935 the figure drawing of 300 Bengali children, aged from six to thirteen years, and found that most of the figures drawn by those under nine years of age were naked, although as many as 20 per cent of the children aged twelve to thirteen also drew naked figures. Although he refrained from making any general observations at the time, he discovered that the most popular parts of the body were forehead, hair, eye, nose, cheek, chin, leg, toe, hand, and fingers.[2]

Of the Ravens Progressive Matrices, H. R. Burke considers them 'as nearly culture-free as any other test is, or can be, but conclusive evidence on that point is lacking'[3]—while Anastasi reflects that 'studies in a number of non-European cultures, however, have raised doubts about the suitability of this test for groups with very dissimilar backgrounds. In such groups, moreover, the test was found to reflect the amount of education, and to be susceptible to considerable practice effect'.[4]

In view of the inconclusive nature of the first tests at Spring Grove, a more detailed study was carried out in 1962 by the educational psychologist and the headmaster, in an endeavour to assess the educational potential of these children, irrespective of the different opportunities of learning the types of skills found in an English cultural environment. All Indian and Pakistani children, including those already integrated in the main school, and the non-integrated, were once again given the Ravens Progressive Matrices and the Goodenough 'Draw a Man' test.

In addition to these tests, for purposes of comparison, the teachers of the originally non-English-speaking children, who were now integrated, were asked to record the school attainments

---

[1] P. L. Shrimali, *The Standardization of the Goodenough Intelligence Test for India*, Abstracts from *Proceedings* of the 34th Indian Science Congress, 1947, pp. 59–60.

[2] Anathnath Datta, 'Drawings of Children', *Indian Journal of Psychology*, October 1935, pp. 179–82.

[3] H. R. Burke, 'Ravens' Progressive Matrices: A Review and Critical Evaluation', in *J. Genet. Psychology*, 1958, pp. 93, 199–228.

[4] A. Anastasi, *Psychological Testing*, New York, Macmillan, 2nd ed., 1961, p. 261.

F

of these children as compared with the standards attained by the normal population of the school (Table 1).

TABLE 1

School Attainments of Integrated Immigrants (N = 45) as compared with Standards attained by the Normal Population of the School (N = 143)—March 1963

	Number	Reading	Writing	Written Free Expression	Spelling	Drawing (Detail & Accuracy)	General Bodily Co-ordination: P.E. & Games
Above average	17·8 (8)	15·6 (7)	15·6 (7)	13·2 (5)	17·8 (8)	8·8 (4)	13·3 (6)
Average	28·9 (13)	31·1 (14)	53·3 (24)	26·3 (10)	20·0 (9)	51·2 (23)	51·2 (23)
Below average	53·3 (24)	53·3 (24)	31·1 (14)	60·5 (30)	62·8 (28)	40·0 (18)	35·5 (16)

TABLE 2

Non-Verbal Intelligence Tests Results of Non-Integrated and Integrated Indian and Pakistani Children—1962

Class	Goodenough		Ravens	
	N =	Av. I.Q.	N =	Below 5th Percentile
Special English 1	14	67	14	10
Special English 2	10	70	5	4
Special English 3	12	76	12	11
Integrated children Junior 1–Junior 4	20	83	20	7

Of the two tests taken, the Goodenough test (Table 2) perhaps presented the least difficulty, and since the teachers' estimates indicated that the majority of integrated children were of average, or above average, drawing ability, it was assumed that they would not find the task of drawing a man either too difficult or completely alien to them.

The results suggested that as the non-English-speaking child moves nearer to becoming integrated, his measurable level of non-verbal intelligence changes from that of an educationally subnormal child, to that of dull or low average intelligence, thus indicating the inaccuracy of the test when applied to children newly arrived.

It is, perhaps, coincidental—even fortuitous—that the increase in non-verbal intelligence occurs at the same time as this improvement. It would be incorrect, however, to equate non-verbal intelligence increases with teachers' decisions to transfer each child, as these decisions are based on a subjective estimate of improvement in general all-round educational ability, with the emphasis laid mainly on proficiency in English.

The 'Man' drawings of the children tended largely to support the observations of Datta, in that the items in which success was most often obtained involved representations of a head, trunk, arms, legs, eyes, nose, mouth, and fingers—with the exception of the last item, the conventional matchstick figures.

One inference from these results is that the children have been handicapped by previous lack of opportunity for drawing and restriction placed on creativeness in their home environment.

The generally low results of the Ravens test (Table 2) suggested that possibly the degree of perceptual maturity which is required for accurate problem-solving with the matrices was too great. Possibly, too, the children were not accustomed to seeing regular coloured geometrical patterns or designs in their previous home environment. The simpler tests were solved by most, with a gradual decline as the problems grew more difficult.

Following the tests, an attempt was made to relate each teacher's rankings of his children's 'general educational ability' to the results of the Goodenough and Ravens assessments. A study of all the information underlined a closer relationship between teachers' rankings of educational ability and the Ravens matrices than with the Goodenough rankings (Table 3).

As there seems to be a progressive lessening of relationship with the Goodenough rankings as the children become 'integrated' it would appear that, as other skills are mastered, drawing loses some of its importance as a means of expression and transfer of thoughts and ideas. However, there does not appear to be a very close relationship between measures of non-verbal intelligence and educational ability. We may infer that

TABLE 3

Children in Table 2 ranked by Teachers according to General Educational Ability correlated (Rho) with Goodenough and Ravens ranks

	Special English 1	Special English 2	Special English 3	Integrated Children J1–J4
Ravens V Teachers' Rank	·458	·829	·521	·597
Goodenough V Teachers' Rank	·887	·358	·179	·035

such ability is mainly verbal, and does not correspond closely to the kind of intelligence measured by the Goodenough and Ravens tests.

Table 1 compares the attainments of the newly integrated immigrants with those of the other children of the main school and it is noticeable that the majority of the integrated immigrants fall in the 'below average' category. Table 2 implies a progressive increase in the level of 'intelligence' (as measured by the criteria set forth by Goodenough, 1926) with increased age and proficiency on the part of the immigrants. It will be seen that only 35 per cent of the sample of integrated children score in the lowest category (at or below the fifth percentile) whereas 71 per cent, 80 per cent, and 92 per cent of the sample score in this category in Special English classes one, two, and three, respectively. Table 3 suggests that the Ravens test result would, in general, agree rather more than 50 per cent with what teachers estimate to be the general educational ability of this sample of immigrant children—not a very close agreement. Whilst the Goodenough results agree closely—almost 90 per cent—with teachers' estimates when the children are newly arrived and non-English-speaking, this agreement falls off steeply with increased age and educational proficiency.

Of the children tested in 1961, three-quarters showed an average increase of thirteen Goodenough I.Q. points when re-tested six months later in 1962. The scores indicate a tendency to move out of the 'E.S.N.' grouping and up into the 'dull' category. It must be observed, however, that the Ravens matrices scores show no such increase. It is interesting to note that scores in an extensively administered test to seventy-one matched pairs, five-year-olds, of West Indian immigrant children and English children, showed no significant differences.[1] The tests used in this case were more culture-free than the Goodenough and other tests mentioned above.

When reviewing test scores, note should be taken of the word of caution implied in the UNESCO 'Statement on Race'[2] which affirms:

It is now generally recognized that intelligence tests do not in themselves enable us to differentiate safely between what is due to innate capacity and what is the result of environmental influences, training and education. Whenever it has been possible to make allowances for differences in environmental opportunities, the tests have shown essential similarity in mental characteristics in all human groups.

From the time that Spring Grove was reorganized to cater for the education of non-English-speaking children until this year, none of the immigrant children had been directly selected for Grammar school. However, three children—a Latvian girl, a Sikh boy, and a Pakistani boy—have been selected for a Grammar school education as a result of the 'Late Developer' tests, organized annually by the Huddersfield Education Authority. Each of these children undertook the tests at their different Secondary Modern schools within four terms of leaving Spring Grove following the normal Secondary selection procedure.

The Sikh boy, Balhar, who was one of our early scholars, continued with his Special English 'tutorials' at our school during his first six months at the Secondary Modern school, and the Pakistani boy, Iftakhar, produced some outstanding results in his 'Late Developer' examination. This boy took the two non-verbal tests mentioned earlier, obtaining a rating of 'definitely above the average in intellectual capacity' on the Ravens test. On the Goodenough test, however, his score was almost down to the educationally subnormal level.

It is obvious that the limited time available to these children, from their admission at nine years of age, without any knowledge of the English language, to the process of Secondary selection between ten and eleven years, handicapped them

[1] See article by V. P. Houghton in *Race*, Vol. VIII, No. 2, October 1966.
[2] UNESCO, *The Race Concept* (Paris, 1952), pp. 98–108.

severely, particularly where language was involved in the tests used. For even well-integrated children who are able to express themselves perfectly adequately lack a wide enough vocabulary when asked to give three other words meaning 'fast'. They have not been conditioned by years of passive assimilation of the English language to be able to paraphrase or to make a statement in more than one way.

There were Pakistani and Indian children in the local Grammar schools in the early years of our scheme, but they had been attending other Grammar schools before coming to Huddersfield, so presumably there had been no language problem.

The academic year commencing in September 1963 saw the first successes under the direct transfer scheme to Grammar school as a result of the Secondary selection tests. In Huddersfield these tests consist of nine separate examinations, from November to the following March, made up of three papers in arithmetic, three in English, and three in verbal reasoning.

Whereas in the past purely academic achievements have been limited to the three scholars previously mentioned, and to several of our former immigrant pupils who have been awarded progress prizes at their Secondary schools, in 1964 two boys who were completely non-English-speaking when they entered the school were selected for a Grammar school. Furthermore, at another local Primary school, Srindar, an Indian girl who had spent the first four years of her English Primary education at Spring Grove, prior to transfer there under our scheme, has also been selected to go to a Grammar school.

Although we do not measure the success or lack of success of our system at Spring Grove by academic achievements alone, we are indeed proud of these children. Our two boys were Roman, a Ukrainian boy, who joined us at the age of five unable to speak English, and Rajan, a Sikh, who came to the school only two and a half years ago, also with no knowledge of the English language. We consider both these boys extremely intelligent but an interesting comparison can be drawn from their I.Q. range and the ratings from the Ravens and Goodenough tests. Roman's I.Q. rating was in grouping of 135 and over and his assessment from the Ravens and Goodenough tests was 'high intellectual capacity' whilst Rajan registered an I.Q.

in the grouping 110–115 with his Ravens and Goodenough rating being 'intellectually average'.

Although these results encourage us, we still believe that the majority of immigrant children who arrive at Junior school age are definitely handicapped, particularly where selection is dependent upon written language work. The Huddersfield Education Authority's 'Late Developer' system, however, does give these children a further opportunity, and quite often the extra time available does allow them to improve their written and spoken English in the less exacting and demanding atmosphere of the Secondary Modern school.

We have been fortunate in our liaison with the local Secondary Modern schools in that we have always maintained close contact and the progress of each immigrant child has received excellent follow-up treatment after transfer at eleven years of age.

The transfer procedure to Secondary schools, in addition to the selection tests, requires that the head teacher of each Junior school should place all boys and girls of selection age on a list in order of merit, the list to be submitted to the Local Education Authority. At Spring Grove we amend our list by indicating three additional categories in which we place our non-English-speaking children of Secondary selection age.

In the first category are children who have passed through the Special English department and have been transferred to a normal Junior school class. They are required to take the tests, for although they have been in school for less time than their class-mates, we feel that this is only fair to the English children.

In the second category are placed those children in the Special English department who are considered to be suitable for testing towards the end of the school year, that is in about the month of June.

The third list contains children in the Special English department whom we consider are not ready to undertake any type of test owing to their complete lack of knowledge of the English language. The children in this category are usually transferred at a later date to the appropriate Secondary schools in a similar manner to those who arrive at Spring Grove after their eleventh birthday.

We are often asked if our special problems and the unusual

TABLE 4

Secondary Selection Results before and after 1958

1952–53	12 selected for Grammar school out of 36 $= 33 \cdot 3\%$	
1953–54	9 ,, ,, ,, ,, ,, ,, 41 $= 21 \cdot 9\%$	
1954–55	14 ,, ,, ,, ,, ,, ,, 73 $= 19 \cdot 2\%$	Average
1955–56	9 ,, ,, ,, ,, ,, ,, 38 $= 23 \cdot 7\%$	23%
1956–57	11 ,, ,, ,, ,, ,, ,, 50 $= 22\%$	
1957–58	8 ,, ,, ,, ,, ,, ,, 44 $= 18\%$	
1958–59	6 ,, ,, ,, ,, ,, ,, 36 $= 16 \cdot 6\%$	
1959–60	7 ,, ,, ,, ,, ,, ,, 34 $= 20 \cdot 5\%$	
1960–61	5 ,, ,, ,, ,, ,, ,, 20 $= 25\%$	Average
1961–62	7 ,, ,, ,, ,, ,, ,, 30 $= 23 \cdot 3\%$	22%
1962–63	6 ,, ,, ,, ,, ,, ,, 30 $= 20\%$	
1963–64	9 ,, ,, ,, ,, ,, ,, 35 $= 25 \cdot 7\%$	

nature of our work reduce the chances of the English children when they are faced with Secondary selection tests. On the contrary, we believe that all our children have received the best possible opportunities to benefit in every way from being part of a multiracial community. Our Secondary selection results before and after 1958 show little variation (see Table 4), and the results in 1964, in particular, indicated no holding back academically of the English children. We think that English parents realize the advantages offered by smaller classes, increased staff, and group or individual teaching, and are appreciative of these opportunities. Furthermore, there has never been any expression by parents to the headmaster, indicating that the school might be classified as a coloured one.

CHAPTER IX
OUTSIDE ASSISTANCE

In the early days of our Special English scheme there were few books or aids available to us other than those we made ourselves, or the adaptations we made of books and apparatus used in an ordinary Primary school. Although it was apparent that considerable research had been undertaken, particularly in English language teaching for schools overseas, the publications we studied were mainly textbooks for teachers and books that could be used for adults. The staff made good use of these to familiarize themselves with the methods but, unfortunately, there were no class-books for the children to use or apparatus which could help them. Our methods were evolved by trial and error, preserving what we found to be good and useful, and discarding the ineffectual and time-wasting.

Increasing help has been received from a variety of ancillary services, for which we have always been grateful. As most of the social services in the town eventually became involved in the process of integrating the newcomers, they sought our advice and, in turn, assisted us wherever and whenever possible. However, over the years we have received very little constructive help from sources outside the borough but there have been a few notable exceptions.

It has been interesting to compare our own experience with that of a Canadian school containing many immigrant children. Strathearn School seemed similar to Spring Grove from some points of view, since it was situated in a central down-town district of Montreal. It was a larger school than ours, however, having over 500 pupils representing some twenty-six nationalities, and serving what was a transient community where foreign families settled until they found work and became familiar with Canadian ways. Our own school has 250 children made up of fifteen nationalities.

The range of the economic background of the Canadian

children was much wider than ours, varying from families looked after by welfare funds, to middle-class families with adequate means, and children of university students from all over the world, on fellowships and scholarships at the nearby McGill University.

It was interesting to note that although many nationalitiés were represented, a large number of the Canadian school's children had been born in Canada, and that in spite of this, pride in national background was perpetuating the various mother tongues. This tendency has also proved to be one of our major difficulties.

We were much impressed by the far-sighted generosity of the Canadian Citizenship Branch in Ottawa which provided immigrants, free of charge, with a complete set of books entitled 'Learning the English Language'. The series consisted of four graded textbooks coupled with four pupils' work books, and a most informative teacher's guide, which outlined a plan of the course and gave practical hints and details of teaching procedure. Published by Thomas Nelson in Toronto, the series was produced under the direction of the English Language Research Inc. of Cambridge, Massachusetts. The Canadian branch of Thomas Nelson have also published two work books based on *English through Pictures*, and *English for Newcomers*—a two-volume course for 'New Canadians'. Unfortunately, no central authority has felt the need for similar aids for 'New Britons'.

Since Australia is host to many thousands of immigrants, we felt that an approach to education authorities there for advice might be fruitful, and early in 1963 we received from the Acting Director of Education in Sydney, a parcel of books entitled 'English for Newcomers to Australia'. Whilst these were mainly for adults, we were able to glean some practical help from them, and a careful study showed us that much of the method advocated was already in use at Spring Grove. We therefore felt reassurance that our pioneering approach had been following roughly the right lines.

The inauguration in September 1961, at Leeds University, of a postgraduate Diploma course in the teaching of English as a Second Language, was the first opportunity, at local or regional level, for us to gain some guidance and assistance in tackling an ever-increasing problem. It provided us, too, with the first indication of the awareness held by other people in this country that the rapid increase in immigration must necessarily produce an increase in the numbers of non-English-speaking children in our schools. This awareness was, for some years, lacking in educational circles, whilst being strongly emphasized in other fields such as medical work, housing, social welfare, and employment.

The postgraduate Diploma course at Leeds was taken by students of the Contemporary English Department under the leadership of Professor Strevens, who, at that time, held the Chair of Contemporary English. Members of staff at Spring Grove have been able to attend lectures at Leeds on linguistics, phonetics, and other aspects of second-language teaching, and were among the first guests to be invited to see the Leeds University language laboratory shortly after its installation.

More recently we have benefited even further by having two students who had gained their diploma in the teaching of English as a Second Language, appointed to the teaching staff of the Special English department at Spring Grove. These were certainly the first two men so qualified to undertake specialist work of this nature in our area, if not in the whole country. Previously, students successful in their postgraduate course had found employment overseas, usually under the auspices of the British Council. One of the graduates, however, had his interest aroused when Professor Strevens 'loaned' him to us for experimental work in producing material for teaching English as a foreign language on twin-track tapes. In all, three students from Leeds University, one each year, helped us towards the end of their course. The fact that each of them was a man, proved to be most useful, as there has always been a heavier proportion of boys to girls in the Special English department, whilst the staffing ratio is heavily weighted in favour of women teachers, as in any Primary school.

In return, we have been able to provide the university's Contemporary English Department with a near-at-hand, ready-made training and testing ground for intending teacheis of non-English-speaking children. Although some of their school practice is undertaken in Spain, much of the students' observation time, and their final assessments, have been carried out at

Spring Grove. The department has shown great interest in our experiments and through the students we have made valued contacts in educational circles all over the world.

A similar, but not quite so extensive, link was established with the Faculty of Education at Manchester University, where there is also a Diploma course in the Teaching of English Overseas, and where more recently a short evening course has been successfully run in the field of teaching English to non-English-speaking children.

The Senior Lecturer-in-Charge has always been very helpful, and, in the early days of our experiment, sent us a report of a comparative study he had made of the immigrant children attending schools in Bolton, and we were able to draw some interesting comparisons between the Indian children there and those in our own area. More recently he has brought teachers of immigrant children in the Lancashire area, attending the course in English-teaching, to visit our school, and further interchange of ideas, methods, and materials has taken place.

We have derived much practical benefit from a link with the B.B.C. Educational Recordings Department, which in 1963 expressed an interest in our audio-visual work. It was agreed that Spring Grove should act as an experimental testing ground for audio-visual material which had been specially prepared for use to teach English over the Uganda Radio Network, and tapes, visual aids, and teachers' notes for this new series were loaned to us to enable us to test the reaction of a large group of non-English-speaking children of varying abilities, ages, and aptitudes. Several teachers have found the series most effective when used on an ordinary tape-recorder in a familiar classroom situation. There is sufficient material for a year's work, and it is a pleasure to hear about the activities of the two central figures, the African Sarah and Joseph, instead of the more familiar Janet and John. Whilst the material has obviously been selected with an African cultural background, the situations are everyday ones and are adaptable. A most pleasing and engaging feature is the frequent use of a melodic intonation-pattern, electronically produced, whereby the children hear the 'time' of the words repeated as music and can then remember the rhythmic rise and fall of the words. However, it was felt that for any tape to be really successful it would have to be based on the everyday environment of the children using it and made in the English language the children would use in their normal daily life. Careful preparation would have to ensure that alien features were excluded and that meaningful situations—such as kitchen scenes in which *chapatis* appeared —were included.

We have gained considerable benefit from visits to educational authorities and schools in other parts of the country where problems exist similar in nature to ours, though these visits have only taken place more recently. We have been able to exchange ideas about materials, methods, and equipment, and have taken the opportunity to view the problem in its wider aspects. Each area is affected in a slightly different way, and methods of approach of necessity have to vary to suit the situation locally. The solutions adopted are dependent on whether immigrants have settled in one concentrated area of a town, as in Huddersfield, or whether they are spread out over a large area, as in Birmingham.

In Birmingham, the Education Authority, after surveying the position, decided that the most satisfactory approach was to use a team of peripatetic teachers of immigrant children, who specialize in the teaching of English.

Visits to several schools of the London County Council and the Middlesex Education Authority enabled us to observe their approach to children from overseas. It was interesting to note the varying problems presented by children of a vastly different culture to that of our immigrant children, and, in particular, the attitudes of the Greek and Turkish Cypriots during the political trouble in Cyprus. They were noticeably excitable, and local and national antagonisms had to be contended with when our national Press favoured one side or the other in any dispute. It was here, too, that we became aware of the difference between the percentage of English-speaking immigrant children from the West Indies and Africa and the percentage of immigrant children who speak no English. Obviously, the second group present the greatest problem to the host area, and yet nationally the two groups are classed together as merely 'immigrant' and this can cause confusion.

It appeared that the 'big-city' aggressiveness, seemingly common to all children living in large conurbations, was

aggravated amongst children (and adults) who, for one reason
or another, were discontented and unsettled. Racial antagon-
ism seemed very near to the surface, and the attitude of people
in authority did not seem to be so farsighted and co-operative
as that of the authorities in our own area.

A notable feature, however, of the work undertaken by the
Greater London Council is the provision of a Voluntary Child
Care Committee for each school, with approximately half a
dozen such committees, each being organized and linked together by a paid social worker. This impressed us as being of
great value, both to children and their families, and to the
school staff.

All this information and such helpful advice have had to be
collected and assimilated piecemeal, and are dependent upon
the time and energy of the staff concerned, and on the support
of the Local Education Authority, together with generous
leave of absence and payment of expenses. The Huddersfield
Education Authority has always given the fullest support to our
work, and (what is more important) has allowed us a virtually
free hand in the way we have tackled the education—in the
fullest possible meaning of the word—of the immigrant child.
Whilst allowing us to use our discretion in organizing the work
of the school, our local authority has always taken a keen
interest in our efforts and full consultation has always taken
place when policy has needed formulating and major issues
have been at stake. They have been as generous as possible
with staff allocations, extra money allowed for each child,
equipment—especially audio-visual material—and with leave
of absence to visit places using audio-visual techniques in
modern language teaching.

They have also been most understanding of the fact that the
arrival of immigrant children in large numbers increases the
administrative work of an ordinary school many times over,
and the provision, in recent months, of full-time secretarial
help has made our work run far more smoothly. Problems of
passport and age discrepancies, letters home in English and a
variety of first languages, and countless duplication of ordinary,
everyday school activities, are time-consuming and could not
possibly be dealt with satisfactorily without a full-time secretary.

Because there is no social welfare worker dealing specifically with problems concerning immigrants, the very necessary link between the homes of our children and the school has had to be established and maintained by the local authority's Education and Child Welfare Officers. The multiplicity of social problems presented by an immigrant family in strange surroundings is aggravated by language problems, and by an attitude of fear and suspicion on the part of the immigrants to anyone in authority, and, therefore, our Welfare Officers are to be commended for their sympathetic and persevering efforts to solve problems which would not normally be part of their duty. Fortunately it is possible to see the humorous side of some of these situations, as in the case of a ten-year-old Indian girl, Zasbinder, who had been absent from school for some weeks after an appendix operation. Our Welfare Officer visited the home and Zasbinder, who had been a pupil here for several years and was quite fluent in her spoken English, acted as an interpreter on behalf of her mother. Zasbinder's rather 'sing-song' intonation and our Welfare Officer's Irish brogue resulted in the following comment on the weekly absence slip: 'The girl is recovering from an apparition'!

Close co-operation between the school and all other branches of the Huddersfield Education Department has always played an important part in our work at Spring Grove. We have benefited from our liaison with the educational psychologist, and the services of the local audiologist and speech therapist have always been available to test the hearing of newcomers as soon as possible after reception. With non-English-speaking children it is always wise to make an early check as to whether they appear not to be listening because they do not understand, or because they cannot hear. A factor which must be recognized is the uncanny ability these children have of 'shutting themselves off' from anyone else if they do not want to hear. An old Yorkshire saying has it that: 'There's noan so deaf as don't want to hear', and in this respect they have quickly acquired a Yorkshire habit. Understandably immigrant children have presented various problems in the testing of their hearing, due not only to lack of English, but also to their unfamiliarity with mechanical appliances. Wherever possible a standardized speech discrimination test in English was given, and it was regarded as accurate, but with the majority of our children it was not possible, so was not even attempted. The pure-tone audiograms on the children who understood English were regarded as accurate to within five decibels, but with children whose English was poor or non-existent, the audiograms were regarded merely as an indication of 'hearing difficulty' rather than a correct measurement.

As so much of our work and interest lies in the field of furthering complete integration, it is highly desirable to have not only the co-operation but also the interest of the medical authorities of the town. Again we have been most fortunate in the support we have received at all times, and this was extremely valuable during the smallpox outbreak in the spring of 1962. Although, at first, the parents of our non-English-speaking children did not attend the medical examinations of their sons and daughters, they are now beginning to join us on these occasions, and our older children are most reliable interpreters. The Health Department soon became interested in our immigrant children and the differing problems presented in the schools, and initiated bone-formation checks in an attempt to arrive at more correct ages for some of the children, than those indicated by their passports. This close link with the department has enabled us to make a progressive step forward in the reception procedure, for now all new arrivals from overseas are medically examined, where possible, within forty-eight hours of their arrival at school. This, we feel, is essential considering the home conditions of some of the immigrant children, and should facilitate the early detection of any infectious or contagious disease. Prior to this arrangement we had occasional periods of anxiety, as for instance when a fifteen-year-old boy was found to have very advanced tuberculosis when he had already been in school for two months and had been mixing freely with all the other children.

As we have recently been admitting boys and girls from India and Pakistán aged about fourteen years, and as the parents of these children have wished them to leave school at the statutory leaving age of fifteen, it has been necessary for several of them to take up jobs directly from Spring Grove. Here the local Youth Employment Department has been most useful, and its officers have made every effort to ensure that our school-leavers have obtained work. The procedure followed has included one or more visits to the school by a Youth Employment Officer to interview our 'leavers', and then investigations have been carried out into suitable vacancies in the local industries. With children who will be leaving school with only a very limited command of the English language, their successful placing in employment is a very difficult task. One can appreciate the thoughts of an employer who has to consider the question of using another employee to explain many of the techniques, skills, and the vocabulary entailed, to the immigrant beginner. It is not an easy decision for an employer who has his attention focused on efficiency and full production. So far, however, the efforts of our Youth Employment Officers have been successful and again another link in the chain of social integration has been forged.

No attempts at social integration could be successful without the co-operation of interested organizations outside the boundaries of the school. The Girl Guides and Boy Scouts Associations have made efforts to interest our children in their activities, and several have been enrolled. It was a memorable occasion when, for the first time, several of our Indian girls arrived at school in their Girl Guide uniforms.

Some of the boys joined a local branch of the Air Training Corps, and others have been welcomed into Youth Clubs. Mindi even made his teacher a reading lamp for Christmas as a result of his attendance at his Youth Club's woodwork classes. A very welcome extension of the hand of friendship came when one Christmas a local Methodist Youth Group invited all our immigrant children to be their guests at a Christmas party at their chapel. Approximately 75 per cent of our immigrant children accepted the invitation, were transported to and from the party by coach, were entertained to tea and games, and received a visit from Father Christmas.

Other more adult bodies have expressed an interest in the work of the school, and this has manifested itself in innumerable invitations to the headmaster and members of staff to address various associations about the work and successes of a multi-racial school. This is a vital part of the integration process and enables us to ensure that an ever-growing number of people are encouraged to believe in the ultimate and lasting value of such a venture.

G

Help from outside has shown itself in many ways, and one of the most important from the child's point of view is the support given to our efforts by other schools with their follow-up work on receiving our pupils. Our work would have lost some of its value if other Primary and Secondary schools had not shown they were prepared to continue the rather special approach academically, and to give every encouragement to those engaged in the task of equipping these young people both socially and emotionally to fit in to our community.

No finer lead has been given in this direction than that of Royds Hall Secondary school, which has taken the largest proportion of children transferred at Secondary age. On leaving Spring Grove the children have been admitted to special remedial groups. The teacher in charge of this remedial department has always taken a special interest in our work, and has attempted to follow up the methods we have used in order to maintain continuity, and to ensure that these children do not lose the confidence gained at Spring Grove. Even while they were still at our school, facilities for older boys and girls to attend woodwork and cookery lessons were readily made available at Royds Hall.

In the near future, when all non-English-speaking children of Secondary age are gathered together in a reception language centre at a mixed Secondary Modern school, it is only fitting that this particular school should have been chosen to fulfil this role.

Because of the keen interest in our experiment evident in various parts of the country—indeed all over the world—visitors to Spring Grove are a regular feature of our life. Educational experts, sociologists, and many others have come from as far afield as Kenya, Swaziland, Turkey, Trinidad, Japan, Iceland, the Philippines, Canada, Nigeria, Cyprus, Israel, and many European countries, and many representatives of education authorities and other bodies in this country have also visited the school. They have been most welcome, and the interchange of ideas that has resulted can only have been beneficial. Although we have regular visiting days we endeavour to disturb the children as little as possible, and by careful planning they have come to regard the visits as part of the routine. At a more domestic level, our caretakers and cleaning staff at all times have been most patient and helpful, and have played an important role in the social integration of our children.

Throughout these days of experimenting, of accepting or discarding, of formulating and pioneering, help and guidance from the Ministry of Education, now the Department of Education and Science, has only occasionally been in evidence. This might possibly be because the education of immigrant children is a completely new field. However, six years is a considerable time, and our experiences have shown that the problem shows no sign of decreasing in size. Discussion with colleagues who have been faced with similar problems show complete agreement that a strong lead from the 'top' is vitally necessary. However, 1963 saw the publication, by the Ministry of Education, of a booklet entitled *English for Immigrants*, which gives a broad outline of the problem nationally and is a welcome step forward in the right direction.

CHAPTER X

WEST INDIAN CHILDREN

So far we have described only our work with Asian pupils, but in evaluating the problems involved in the education of immigrant children it is not widely realized that West Indians have real language difficulties in that many of them speak 'folk' or 'Creole' English. Although their problem is different from that of the completely non-English-speaking child, it nevertheless provides a serious obstacle to the complete adjustment of these children in an English educational environment.

Many people may at one time or another have experienced considerable difficulty in understanding a West Indian, particularly if he was agitated or excited. Snatches of conversation overheard between Jamaican workmen on buses, or at the market between their wives, are often incomprehensible to the unattuned ear. On many occasions West Indians have to be passed over for jobs involving contact with the public because they cannot be understood.

Similarly it must have been apparent to any teacher with West Indian children in his class, that not only is their spoken English quite remarkable and unlike Standard English in a number of ways, but also that recent arrivals from the West Indies are slow to understand the spoken word.

When we asked Prudencia, aged nine, from Grenada, if she had found any difficulty in understanding us, she agreed that she had at first, and furthermore indicated that the greatest obstacle was caused by different intonation. Such differences are noticeable, not only in accent and cadence, which alone would make for difficulty in comprehension for the average Englishman, but also to a very marked extent in grammar and vocabulary.

However, it is highly probable that our difficulties in understanding the speech of West Indian children are greater than theirs in understanding us, to the extent that all teachers, and in particular those at Spring Grove because of the nature of the work undertaken here, are skilled in presenting their lessons simply and clearly. They are able to adapt material to suit the needs of the children they teach, and are adept at choosing words and phrases very carefully so as to provide the maximum benefit for those whose knowledge of our language is inadequate.

More troublesome than variations in vocabulary are the grammatical structures used. For example, the misuse of pronouns is as colourful as it is inevitable, and the use of the present tense on all occasions makes for a greatly simplified grammar, but whitens the hair of an English teacher.

On first sight it might seem that these children merely speak 'bad' English, and one is tempted first to condemn, and then evangelically to purify. But it must be remembered that the language they speak is their mother tongue, and is a close relative of the English we speak. Like any other language it has evolved through hundreds of years, being affected by invasions of settlers and traders, and coloured by the wide range of languages spoken by early slaves. In the same way, the English we speak has been moulded, enriched, and enlivened by our history.

Obviously the need for purification is there, for these children will have to be taught to speak and to write orthodox English, if they are to reap any benefit from their education, and if they are to obtain the maximum advantage from being part of an English community when they grow up.

At Spring Grove, when staffing conditions permit, we attempt to give our West Indian children extra English tutorials at regular times in the week, using constructive conversation, rhymes, and oral drills, combined with some written work with the older children. Our aims in general are to encourage clearer and less slipshod articulation in speech, to eliminate common errors of pronunciation (such as 'de' for 'the'), and to create an awareness of tenses, singular and plural verbs, and the correct use of pronouns.

Lessons need very careful preparation beforehand, and much can be achieved with large, colourful, and absorbing wall pictures, or with flannel-graphs. We use stories, repeated and retold orally by the children, and the invention of chain stories starting with an exciting first sentence. Alternatively, general discussion about their own experiences can be fruitful, for, as in all language work, effective teaching must be related to things within the limits of the child's own experience and environment.

Extremely useful, too, are rhymes and jingles, oral games and action songs, all greatly enjoyed by the children. Unfortunately, there is only limited reading material whose content is commensurate with the age level and needs of our West Indians, although we have found the 'Words Together' series[1] most useful in helping to counter grammatical deficiencies peculiar to Creole English.

It is essential for these children to hear a good standard of spoken English from all those with whom they come into contact. Thus, much of the teachers' work can be nullified when the children go into the playground. One of the common grammatical faults among West Indians is to use singular verbs with plural nouns, and vice versa; for example: 'We was playing marbles' or 'The books is on the table'. Since this is a common fault among less articulate Yorkshire children, the result of immigrant children mixing with English children who do not speak their own language well is not encouraging.

Another handicap is that the English population is gradually moving away from the town centre, and being replaced by immigrant families, making it much more likely that, out of school hours, children who need plenty of opportunity to absorb English at play will be mixing with children of their own race, or who have similar language problems. They are not having enough daily opportunities to extend their vocabulary and widen their horizons.

English children tend to have three grades of speech—that of the home, that of the street and playground, and that of the classroom—but with West Indian children the speech of the street and the home are usually the same. They develop a second grade of speech only when they have been in the settled school environment for a considerable period of time, or when they find that they are not being understood, and make a conscious effort to slow down their flow of conversation and articulate more clearly.

Obviously children of differing age groups need a different

---

[1] J. D. Bentley, *English Language Practice for the West Indies*, London, 1962.

approach in the English tutorials, for while Infant work is almost entirely oral, with Juniors some written work can be of great value. If children arrive in this country at the age of nine or ten, they will need more concentrated attention than those who start school at five, for the five-year-old children will have time in which to adapt and assimilate.

Two main difficulties face the teacher. First, in all probability their families speak the same kind of English as they do, and they will therefore not be receiving the necessary conditioning at home. Secondly, they are in the unenviable position of having to unlearn and eradicate some of the old speech habits acquired from birth, while retaining others; and it must be exceedingly difficult to be bilingual in Standard English and Creole English, although we understand that most educated adult West Indians achieve this quite happily. In this respect Indians and Pakistanis have a less confusing task, because for them it is a question of straight learning.

Sometimes it may appear that the success is infinitesimal when set against the amount of work put in, and the teacher will feel that his or her efforts are in vain. The success, however, even if only limited, is more likely to be noticed by the class teacher, who will benefit from it in a number of ways. In addition to any actual progress in improving the English of the children, regular tutorials enable the class teacher to give time to other children in the class, time which would otherwise be spent on coping with the West Indians.

It is most important to establish a close link between the teacher who is in charge of the tutorial work and the relevant class teacher in order that continuity may be maintained and definite progress made by the individual child. The real carry-over of the work is much enhanced when tutorial teaching is linked, where possible, to class activities.

In Infants' classes it has been noticeable following tutorials that the West Indians are able to participate more fully and more actively in the classroom, being able to understand and make themselves understood. They appear to be better adjusted socially and infinitely more secure in their environment. This social readjustment is most important, since their home background is too often unsettled, and any feeling of security we can give them is of infinite value.

The ability to speak a comprehensible brand of English appears to vary considerably from child to child, and is probably dependent on such factors as whether he was brought up in a large city or in a small rural community, and on the extent of educational background. In general most of our West Indian children come from Jamaica or Grenada, and few from the more progressive island of Trinidad. Therefore, it would seem likely that educational opportunities have been very limited.

Similarly, few of the West Indian immigrants to Huddersfield are professional or middle-class people, making it probable that the children we receive into school will be in the lower ability and intelligence range.

Individually and collectively the West Indian children are happily extrovert, noisy, and full of self-expression. To the unscientific observer they may give the impression of having butterfly minds, and an inability to apply themselves to a given task for any length of time. They appear to find it difficult to take life seriously, and, unfortunately, their often unsettled home backgrounds and lack of parental interest are a serious obstacle to an improvement of their standards within school.

Only on rare occasions have parents been to school to see how their children were progressing, and as a group they seem totally uninterested. If parents have visited school they have been mothers, and we have only received one West Indian father. His approach was to thrash his son every time he felt the desired progress had not been made, and he eventually side-tracked his obligations by sending the boy back to Jamaica.

In comparison with English children they are sadly handicapped when they start school by the lack of pre-school training and activities. Apart from those who come from poor home conditions, most English children learn to hold a pencil or crayons at a very early age, can distinguish colours, can count, or have handled books, toy clocks, construction sets, mosaics, or dolls' houses. Consequently, when they begin their school life they are able to participate quickly in individual or group activities, thus gaining confidence and a feeling of security. Such pre-school training is invaluable to the teacher, for it provides a foundation upon which he or she can build.

The general maltreatment of grammatical structures in West Indian speech decreases as the child gets older and the influence of school is felt, but the process is slow and inevitably not rapid enough to equip him at the appropriate age for competing with English children in many types of selection test. On the other hand, if 'Eleven Plus' examinations were abandoned and head teachers asked to assess the true merits of each child, there is a possibility that there would be better opportunities for this type of child.

On balance it would be safe to say that even the most highly intelligent West Indian child would be handicapped to some extent by his home language in comparison with an English child. For even when an English child has a stunting home environment, it is fairly certain that the English he hears spoken, even if slovenly in articulation and accent, is largely syntactically correct. It is true, however, that large numbers of English children leave school at fifteen having lost none of this slovenly articulation.

With the considerable increase in the numbers of West Indian children being admitted to our classes, it seems that the problem is unlikely to diminish for some time to come. The area which Spring Grove serves is rapidly becoming a popular area for West Indians to settle down, and quite apart from new arrivals to the area, the already established West Indian families are growing rapidly.

While we have our Special English department for non-English-speaking children, we have managed so far to cope with the slightly different West Indian problem by taking out from the regular Primary classes small tutorial groups of eight or nine children at a time.

If, however, the proportion of West Indians grows to any great extent, we may well find ourselves with English children in the minority in ordinary classes. Perhaps then the answer will be to give the tutorial work to the English children, in order that they do not suffer from the general lowering of standards inevitable when large numbers of children with inadequate English are in one class. Much will depend on the continuing generosity of our Local Education Authority in providing people to help with Infant classes. A nursery-trained Infant teacher would help considerably with many of the social problems and training. The situation might also arise where we shall have to consider a re-division of labour at Infant level, and either divide the classes laterally by ability instead of chronologically, or work in 'family' groups.

CHAPTER XI

THE VALUES OF A MULTIRACIAL SCHOOL

One of the most interesting fruits of our experiment has been the excellent relationships that have developed between the children. The knowledge we have gained has not been purely academic, confined to the development of a workable method of teaching a second language. It has given us a deep feeling of satisfaction to learn that children of mixed nationalities can work and play together almost unaware of differences in the colour of skin or style of dress.

The very nature of the school building lends itself to the establishment of an intimate family spirit. Each classroom overlooks the large, old-fashioned chapel-like hall, and the daily activities and movement about the school of the children can be observed by everybody. This has its drawbacks, for physical education or music lessons can be disturbing when their noises infiltrate the classroom doors. On balance the advantages outweigh the disadvantages, and we feel that the atmosphere of good-natured, affectionate unity would not have been so rapidly established if we had occupied an ultra-modern concrete block, with doorways turning off from long, impersonal corridors.

Although we are virtually two schools within one, many of our day-to-day activities are shared; also, wherever possible, members of the Special English staff teach a few lessons a week in the main school, and main-school teachers occasionally teach Special English classes. Much of the needlework in the school is taught by a member of the Special English staff, while art-teaching is the responsibility of a teacher whose timetable is mostly spent in the main school. This interchange of teachers has a double value, both academic and social. Even when originally non-English-speaking children learn our language, it is inevitable that they will to some extent be handicapped throughout their school career, particularly in their command of idiom in reading and written skills. Because all the teachers are aware of this, and are familiar with the problems of individual children, special care is taken in the main school that there is a constructive carry-over of work already begun in the Special English department.

Fortunately, it is also a fact that teachers who work at Spring Grove have chosen voluntarily to teach in a multiracial school, fully understanding the problems, and the differences from normal teaching, involved. They are, therefore, more likely to be fully sympathetic to the social and emotional needs of the children in comparison to those struggling to absorb immigrant children into ordinary English classes without their receiving the benefits of a period of preparation in a centre such as ours.

Our children play together in the playground, and become adept remarkably quickly at reproducing the language of the playground, as well as learning lessons in tolerance and goodwill to those from a different background. They join together for games, school dinners, and morning assembly, giving ample opportunity for children of different nationalities, colours, and religions to mix together. It helps to break down any barriers of reserve that might previously have existed, and in the case of Indian and Pakistani girls it eradicates some of their natural shyness. More Asian children are taking advantage of the school meals service, possibly reassured by the fact that they will not appear conspicuous in a gathering of such varied nationalities. It has been known for immigrant children, who form only a tiny proportion of a school's population, to be too shy and too afraid of seeming different to stay for school dinners.

The multiplicity of religions represented in the school has so far led to no problems, and we accept the fact that Christians, Sikhs, Muslims, and Hindus, although praying jointly, are each praying in a slightly different direction, to their own God. Readings are chosen not only from the Bible, but also from a variety of sources, poems, and prose. The children are always interested in comparing their religions, and the immigrants find our Bible stories stimulating and in keeping with the philosophies instilled by their own cultures, without in any way compromising their faith. Parents too seem to have no conscientious objection to this attitude.

Annual events such as the Harvest Festival, carol service, and bulb show, are enjoyed by English and immigrant children alike, and are especially valuable in that they introduce the Asians to more relaxed and light-hearted school activities, probably unknown in the rigid type of education they received at home. Whenever possible we observe Indian and Pakistani festivals. A particular favourite is the Indian *Diwali*, or Festival of Light, for which we light a hundred or more candles round the hall, and we are entertained by our Asian children with songs and dances in national costume. A highlight of one such celebration occurred when Kazimir, a twelve-year-old Polish boy, and Safdar, a thirteen-year-old Pakistani boy, held hands to sing together 'A happy birthday, India'.

We find that the Western ear gradually becomes attuned to the different tonal system of Asian music, and that music is one part of a real two-way cultural exchange, rather than a conditioning of the immigrant child to our arts and customs, with the host community accepting nothing in return.

On rainy days the school's two admirable dinner supervisors sometimes lead a spontaneous international talent concert, full of contrasting items. Perhaps two little West Indian girls will sway together singing the latest 'pop' song, followed by an Indian boy performing a fiery Indian war song. Then comes a rousing chorus of 'Jesus wants me for a sunbeam', and the whole gathering causes the walls to vibrate while dancing the Hokey Cokey or the Twist.

Christmas festivities are entered into with the greatest enthusiasm by children of all nations. The frenzy of paper-chain-making and classroom-decorating reaches fever pitch in time for the Christmas parties. Greetings cards, painstakingly made, are posted in the school pillar-box for teachers and friends. Often cards are shop-bought, with bizarre results. We have received 'Christmas' cards wishing us 'A Happy Mother's Day', or 'A Happy Wedding Anniversary', and one of the most appealing was sent to a woman teacher, with the printed message, 'A Happy Birthday—you're the tops from any angle!'

This enthusiasm for everything they undertake is typical of our immigrant children, who abound in good nature and happy affection. Yet they have, too, a quiet dignity and resilience of character, which cushions them to the shock of being transplanted overnight, and is an essential ingredient in the success of their adaptation. Behaviour problems are rare, and the Indian and Pakistani children have an amazing capacity for conscientious hard work, which in its turn affects the attitude to work of the English children. Their standard of honesty is the highest, and their generosity overwhelming.

We are fortunate in possessing a large, attractive library of some 2,500 books, and all the children, both English and immigrant, are encouraged to use it freely, for reading, and for such relaxations as chess-playing. This ready availability of books of all kinds, for light reading and for study, plays a valuable part in the cultural integration of our pupils.

Much can be learned about the social customs of the children by watching them closely at work and at play. Many of the games, such as jacks, marbles, and skipping, which are popular with newly arrived Asian children, bear similarities to those played by English children. On the other hand, in the classroom we have been fascinated by the display of domestic routine demonstrated in the 'Wendy house' by the five- and six-year-olds. When playing at 'house', father spends most of his time being offered cups of tea, or lying on a 'divan' being fanned with paper fans by the womenfolk of his family. When playing at 'hospitals', too, one 'nurse' seems to be employed full-time to fan the patients.

Although great reliance is placed by the Asian community on the National Health Service, one eleven-year-old Indian girl was convinced that the stye in her eye was cured not so much by the ointment provided by the school clinic, but by a piece of silk thread tied round her middle toe by her mother. Conversation periods are rich in revelations about the social and family life of our immigrant pupils, and this is gratefully accepted by the teacher as an unostentatious and rewarding way of learning about their culture.

We find that almost all our activities provide lessons in mutual understanding and exchange of ideas. One teacher, describing a lesson with eleven-year-old Junior children, wrote in his record book:

The B.B.C. Schools' programme 'How Things Began' included the funeral of one of the villagers, and mention of an 'after-life' prompted discussion about heaven. We were able to have many interesting exchanges of ideas between our own children and the Muslims. The realization that they differ only in very minor ways, will, I am sure, do nothing but good in integrating future generations. This was one of the occasions which provided real satisfaction in working in a multi-racial school. Such understanding in the past and perhaps the Crusades could have been avoided.

The most important social factor that has emerged from the Spring Grove experiment in multiracial education is the complete lack of colour prejudice among young children. They are almost unaware of colour, and we have found that animosity usually arises only when the prejudices of parents and other adults make themselves felt.

Even in the very early days of the scheme we were delighted to find evidence of what is an essential ingredient of successful integration. One day a little English girl came to the teacher on playground duty, crying that someone had hit her. When asked who it was, she said that she did not know his name, but would be able to point him out. On reaching the classroom, she said immediately, 'It's that boy in the green blazer.' The significant thing was that the boy in the green blazer was also the only coloured child in the room at the time.

English parents have, on the whole, been very sympathetic to our work, and have been kept fully in touch with our aims and the methods we use. In fact on a number of occasions English parents who have moved from the district have specially requested that their children should be allowed to stay on at Spring Grove. It is possibly significant that the area we serve is one where parents are neither school- nor class-conscious. Because we are a multiracial school, immigrant parents are more likely to come to talk to teachers, knowing there will be interpreters available, and having a feeling of 'safety in numbers' which could not be the case if their children were just one or two 'lost' in a large English school.

We have been satisfied that while the proportion of immigrant to English children is well balanced, not only do the English children not suffer in any way from receiving their education in a multiracial school; on the contrary, they benefit greatly from the cultural interchanges and from the tolerant, good-natured relationship which results. In their turn the immigrant children reap the advantages of being able to spend some time in a school whose aim it is to prepare them in every way for their eventual move into an ordinary school, either Secondary or Primary.

In spite of the depressed area from which a considerable number of our English children are drawn, in Secondary selection tests the results have compared favourably with the average for the borough, and we have found it profitable to introduce French for groups of eight-, nine- and ten-year-old children in the main school. As a result a number of immigrant children are now learning their third language, along with their English classmates.

Inevitably, the children, because of their lack of prejudice, are the essential spearhead in the movement for successful integration, and the next and subsequent generations will benefit from work that is being done at the present time.

CHAPTER XII

FUTURE NEEDS

From the developments in Huddersfield in dealing with the education of immigrant children have emerged two clearcut issues needing urgent attention from educationists and sociologists, and above all from the Government. First, greater efforts must be made both nationally and regionally to recognize the needs and difficulties of schools involved in the teaching of English as a Second Language. Strangely enough there are still educationists who refuse to admit that there is a problem at all, some even who insist upon saying 'Ah, yes, but they all know *some* English when they arrive.' This is not at all true, and the majority of immigrant children enter our schools knowing not a single word of our language. The second problem is the much wider one of the general integration of immigrants into the social and cultural structure of their new country. This too, however, is closely linked with education, for the children being educated today in British schools are the adults of tomorrow, and as such will be able to influence the social climate in which they will spend their maturity. In both spheres a great deal of immediate reshaping and replanning is necessary if integration is to be smooth and successful.

In schools where immigrant children are taught the urgent need is for specialist teachers. Until quite recently the teaching of English to non-English-speaking children has been undertaken by teachers who, although dedicated, have been quite unprepared for their task. At last, however, it is being recognized that to teach English as a Second Language is as skilled an occupation as teaching French or Russian. In fact, the new methods and activities advocated for teaching French in Primary schools are similar to those that have proved successful over six years of experiment in teaching English at Spring Grove.

The recruitment of qualified teachers in this field of education

H

can be approached from three directions. Far too many students
are leaving teacher-training colleges completely unaware of the
many problems presented to the young probationer by immigrant children. Occasionally we have received individual re-
quests from final-year students asking if they might visit our
school to observe our methods, having become aware of the
problem, but in general there has been no concerted effort to
recognize the need for specialized training. It would be a great
step forward if training colleges would include in their curriculum a general study of the problems caused by immigrant
children. Even more valuable would be a course on language
teaching for all students. For those training colleges connected
with industrial areas, an optional course in the teaching of
English as a Second Language could well be offered.

A second hunting-ground for recruitment is among existing
teachers. There are those already experienced in the Primary or
Secondary field who have either become interested in immigrant
teaching through reading about it or through contacts with
other schools, or those who are already struggling in the dark
with the difficulties of increasing numbers of non-English-
speaking children in their classes. For these teachers intensive
in-service training should be made available, and could well be
the responsibility of the institutes of education. These institutes
would be linked with the training colleges and the future
teachers, through special courses for lecturers in training
colleges.

A number of universities are now organizing postgraduate
Diploma courses in the teaching of English as a Second Language. These courses can be of great value in the teaching of
English to children provided that not too much emphasis is
placed on linguistics, and that very much more attention is
given to the practical problems of handling a class full of children, of teaching language through activities, and the essential
linking of language teaching with other subjects.

Many young immigrant children will pass through our
schools in the next decade, many of them very young, and a
good supply of nursery-trained teachers should be high on the
list of priorities. We were impressed by the capable handling of
immigrant children of pre-school age by the nursery teachers
at several Inner London Education Authority Primary schools.

In their nurseries the numbers were small and therefore much of the vital social training habits of hygiene and school routine were being dealt with before the children actually entered the Infant departments.

If a constructive effort is made to draw the maximum number of teachers from the sources outlined it will relieve the teachers who have, actually in their classrooms, been training new-comers to this work. Care must still be taken, however, to ensure that the schools are not besieged by an increasing number of well-meaning people who wish to 'dabble' in this new educational topic. The children, always our most important consideration, have their education disturbed enough by visits from educationists and students, which we know are very necessary if establishments similar to our own are to benefit from our experiences, without inroads being made into their lesson time by people conducting research merely to add to their qualifications or to gain information to support a thesis.

Recently we have made increasing use of immigrant teachers, and in particular have found them valuable with the very necessary social training, road-safety, and explanations of school routine. Countless hours of administrative time have been saved through the excellence of their service as interpreters and writers of letters to parents in their own language. Great care must be taken that these teachers have as high a standard of spoken English as possible, that they have had experience of teaching English as a foreign language, and that they are not fanatical in their religious or political beliefs to the extent of their judgement being clouded. Where it is not possible to employ immigrant teachers, it would be useful to have compiled a basic vocabulary in the various languages for the teachers' use in emergencies, and to make for speedier comprehension and reassurance in the early stages while the children are settling down.

From whatever source the teachers are drawn, it is imperative that the Department of Education and Science should be prepared to initiate an immediate and intensive recruitment drive to attract teachers to this arduous but rewarding work. Special incentives should be offered, bearing in mind that immigrant children are handicapped by lack of knowledge of

our language in the same way that deaf, educationally subnormal, and delinquent children are handicapped. It has been
recognized by the Department of Education and Science that
English can be taught successfully only in classes of small
numbers, and in advocating a maximum of twenty pupils per
class, they must also allow that the quota of teachers permitted
to each Local Education Authority be sufficient to meet the
demands of schools with large numbers of immigrant children.
This could be achieved if such schools were treated as special
schools, thus accepting the fact that immigrant children need
special treatment, and at the same time ensuring that teachers
would be attracted financially as well as vocationally. Also those
already giving so generously of their time, energy, and skill
would be justifiably rewarded. Eventually the children will be
able to repay, at least in part, the efforts spent on them by
being able to play a full and productive role in society.

With regard to the ideal maximum number of completely
non-English-speaking children in a class, we have found from
practical experience that fifteen is preferable, after which the
law of diminishing returns applies. Naturally, where comprehension is more advanced the numbers can safely be increased to twenty, but in the initial stages the smaller the group
the better. However, since our experience has been largely with
Asian children we can only relate our estimates to the fact that
for them the acquisition of a new language is doubly difficult,
involving the use of a new script and even a new direction of
writing. Possibly, where the immigrants are Europeans, a
slightly larger number could be dealt with successfully, although
for any language teaching it is vital that there should be ample
opportunity for each child to participate individually, thus
making success more limited with larger numbers.

Full use of audio-visual aids in the past has been handicapped
by lack of suitable tapes for English as a foreign language at
Primary school level. Much successful material has been forthcoming for French and other European languages, but only
very recently has it been realized by publishing firms that the
need for English courses is an urgent necessity. Such equipment
as tape-recorders and even language laboratories is expensive,
as are the training and incentives needed for specialist teachers,
but local authorities must realize that this will be money well

spent. Also untapped, at the time of writing, so far as teaching aids for English to immigrant children are concerned, are sound radio and television, both of which could make an impact with carefully selected material.

One of the more wearying obstacles to successful teaching is the fact that, as we have shown, admissions are not restricted to the beginning of term. Children appear at school to enrol in ones and twos throughout the term, making it not only difficult for the teacher to keep to a progressive scheme of work, but frustrating for children who are already well established in the class and want to get on. It would be a great help if schools were given the power to refuse admission except at the beginning of a term, or even at half-term, so that each class of beginners would start at the same time.

Because the children we teach come from such a different social and cultural background from our own, we feel it important to learn all we can about their native lands, their customs and religions. We have gleaned much from books and what the children themselves have told us, but by far the most valuable enterprise in this respect was the visit made by a member of our staff last summer to the home villages of our Indian and Pakistani children in the Punjab. During his first year of teaching at Spring Grove, this twenty-two-year-old teacher was fascinated by the children and by their culture. The Local Education Authority generously allowed him leave of absence for six months, and he hitch-hiked most of the way to the Jullundur district of the Indian Punjab and the Lahore area of West Pakistan. As well as visiting many schools and educational establishments, he met families and lived in their homes, thus gaining valuable first-hand experience of the customs and character of the Punjabi Indians and Pakistanis. To a number of children his visit had a special magic, for not only did he visit them in their homes last year, but this term was back at Spring Grove in person to welcome them when they arrived with their families, so giving them a feeling of security and familiarity in new circumstances.

Although individual schools and individual education authorities have attempted to deal with the teaching of immigrant children in the manner they felt best suited to their local needs, there has been a regrettable national dilatoriness in accepting this as a problem of some magnitude. Only recently has it been generally acknowledged that a problem exists, while over a period of some years individual schools have been coping with it as well as the shortage of materials, staff, training, and space would allow. Even as recently as early 1963, it was felt at higher levels that a national pooling of ideas and experiences was not necessary, and this at a time when we, amongst others, had been actively engaged in the work for five years. It is, therefore, encouraging to see that now a lead is being given and some enthusiasm engendered.

In order to deal effectively with the variety of problems facing schools up and down the country, the Department of Education and Science should face up squarely to its responsibilities and establish a centre to specialize in dispensing advice and aid on the teaching of English to immigrant children. The setting-up of such a centre would acknowledge that the days of stop-gap measures are over, and it would provide the permanency for which practising teachers in the field have yearned. It must be realized that without effective controls the immigrant school population will increase rather than decrease in the next ten years, and even if the time comes when immigrant children in our schools are mainly English-born, the problem of social integration will still remain.

The values of the centre would be manifold. It should be staffed by linguists, teachers, and sociological experts, as well as able administrators, and should aim among other things at providing a series of courses in the teaching of English as a Second Language to pupils of varying ages and levels of ability. It should give facilities for research into all the many facets of the problem, and act as a storehouse for all the knowledge so gained. Experienced advice in the handling of known teaching materials should be available for all interested teachers, whether in Islington, West Bromwich, or Bradford, and should include texts, audio-visual equipment, flannel-graphs, films, and bibliographies.

This national pooling of ideas about method and equipment is a subject which we are constantly being asked about by visitors to our school, and the centre would seem to provide the solution. The staff could be responsible for research into the different problems involved in teaching reading and writing to

children who are illiterate in their own tongue and teaching it
to those who can already understand a non-Roman script.

It is generally accepted that we are singularly lacking in our
knowledge of methods of testing and assessing the ability of
children on arrival. The need for research into the problem is
most pressing, and if such research proved successful we could
look forward to a time when generally accepted and understood methods of screening, assessment, and placing of pupils
were available, with opportunities for periodic testing and re-
grading. Such a scheme is already in operation in New York in
dealing with Puerto Rican immigrant children.

If a national centre were formed, opportunity would follow
for the establishment of regional centres, with the national body
having a controlling interest. In this way local efforts could be
linked together making the final output more effective.

One field in which the centre or centres could give valuable
help is in the field of youth employment. At present only a
comparatively small number of children from overseas are
filtering out of our schools on to the labour market, and so far
it has been easy for employers to refuse work to these boys and
girls on the grounds of poor ability and lack of knowledge of the
English language. Within the next year or two a far greater
number of immigrant children will be needing employment,
and as a result of their education in our schools over a period of
years, will possess skills equal to those of their English counterparts, and will be fluent in their second language. Immigrant
children with G.C.E. qualifications will need openings which
will allow them to develop their abilities and to further their
education in a variety of jobs, and unless great care is taken
discrimination on the part of the employers or on the part of
trade unions will nullify all the care and hard work that has
been happily given in the schools. Because of this it is vital that
all interested parties should find a common meeting ground to
discuss the problems that are likely to arise—the local councils,
employers, unions, welfare officers, headmasters, and youth
workers. This should be undertaken at once in order to be
prepared, rather than attempting to deal with difficulties piecemeal when they arise in a few years' time.

There will, of course, always be the children who arrive in
this country at the age of fourteen or fifteen with no knowledge

of English, and for them oral fluency must be aimed at above
all else. They need help especially with the language of work,
and to a great extent further education establishments must be
prepared to cater for the needs of school-leavers and children
who do not arrive in this country until the age of fifteen or over,
and who need practical preparation in the language of the
various trades.

The problems affecting school-leavers are only a small part
of the difficulties in welfare matters which arise when there is a
large immigrant community. There is a desperate need in the
affected areas for a liaison officer or committee, to advise on
social matters, to assist in smooth integration and thus to protect
the interests of both residents and immigrant groups. Certainly
we in the schools would feel the immediate benefit if such a post
were to be established in this area, but so far the town council
has steadfastly set its face against such a move. Alternatively, if it
is not considered desirable to appoint an officer to deal with the
social problems of immigrants, the Greater London Council's
system of Child Care Committees springs to mind as worthy of
greater consideration. Whichever method were adopted, it
would serve to ease the burden and release the pressure being
put on all teachers who have to deal with increasing numbers of
immigrant children. Much time is now wasted on purely routine
and administrative work which could be handled efficiently by
these people, and interpreters could be made available to help
with the thousand and one queries which arise in the course of
a school week. In some cases, particularly in London, children
of immigrant parents have arrived at school ill or injured,
having received no attention at home. Again, the children have
sometimes been very hazy as to the whereabouts of their parents
during the day. Hours of a teacher's valuable time may be taken
up searching for a parent who, when found, fights shy of official
authority. This time could well be saved by the employment of
a paid welfare worker who, if unable to overcome the language
barrier, would at least be able to get in touch with appropriate
interpreters.

The link between all interested workers in this branch of the
welfare services could be provided by a newsletter or regular
bulletins from the national and regional centres which would
give teachers, administrators, and welfare workers the most up-

to-date information on developments affecting the education, employment, and welfare of the immigrant population. One feature of such a publication could be current evidence of the figures of admission of all immigrants into the country. If these could be further broken down to supply local statistics, future needs for planning could be estimated in advance.

Although national and regional centres would be largely instrumental in co-ordinating ideas and practical policies in the education of immigrant children and young people, evening institutes and departments of extra-mural studies could be responsible for organizing courses for adult immigrants, with special emphasis upon the females of the group, who are usually the last, by a long way, to adopt a new language.

The problem of the immigrants, however, is in need of a new and sensible approach. From a practical point of view a compulsory health check on all immigrants entering the country would be beneficial to all concerned. There should be opportunities for periodic limiting of numbers entering the country in order to give social services, housing authorities, and education authorities a necessary breathing space. Above all legislation should be introduced to tighten up the regulations governing passports and work permits.

But apart from practical administrative details, the greatest national need is to provide the immigrant with a special service, to give assistance with interpreters, advice on banking facilities, hospital treatment, and the benefits of our social services. Help could be given with employment, housing, and other financial problems such as arise from the intricacies of taxation. General education in citizenship would be available, with explanations of our political and social customs, while overseas teachers and students could be enlisted to help reduce racial prejudice in local areas. The aim should be to establish a central place in each large conurbation, to which all immigrants would have access, staffed by trained officers with a warm, human approach to the problem of absorbing the immigrant as quickly and as happily as possible into the community.

Meanwhile, in the schools, we should continue the process of educating the children and doing our best to integrate them socially and emotionally, whilst at the same time maintaining the ethos of a normal English school. To achieve our aim it is essential that the balance of immigrant to English children within the school should not exceed fifty : fifty, and for maximum benefit it should be no higher than thirty-three and one-third to sixty-six and two-thirds. It is essential, too, that there should be sufficient English children of a high enough level of ability at which the integrated children can aim, in order to achieve a fully balanced multiracial society in the future.

BIBLIOGRAPHY

The following books have been found particularly useful for work with immigrant children:

1. TEACHERS' REFERENCE BOOKS

Allen, W. Stannard, *Living English Structure*, London, Longmans, 1959

Bentley, J. D., *English Language Practice for the West Indies*, London, Hulton, 1962

Cassidy, F. G., *Jamaica Talk*, London, Macmillan, 1962

Clarke, Edith, *My Mother Who Fathered Me*, London, Allen & Unwin, 1957

Desai, R., *Indian Immigrants in Britain*, London, Oxford University Press for the Institute of Race Relations, 1963

Gatenby, E. V., *Direct Method English Course*, London, Longmans, 1953

Hawkes, N., *Immigrant Children in British Schools*, London, Pall Mall Press for Institute of Race Relations, 1966

Hornby, A. S., *The Teaching of Structural Word and Sentence Patterns*, London, Oxford University Press, 1962

Ministry of Education, *English for Immigrants*, London, H.M.S.O., 1963

Palmer, H. E. and D., *English Through Actions*, London, Longmans, 1959

2. READING AND WRITING TEXTBOOKS

Keir, Gertrude, *Adventures in Reading* and *Adventures in Writing*, London, Oxford University Press, 1946; *More Adventures in Reading* and *More Adventures in Writing*, London, Oxford University Press, 1949

O'Hagan, C., *'Peak' Series for Asian Children*, London, Oxford University Press, 1962

3. READING BOOKS

Carver, C., and Stowasser, C. H., *Oxford Colour Reading Books*, London, Oxford University Press, 1963

Federal Readers, The, London, Collins, 1960

Ladybird Books, Loughborough, Wills & Hepworth, 1965

Pattison, B., *New Nation English*, London, Nelson, from 1958

Reading with Rhythm, London, Longmans, 1961

Tansley, A. E., and Nicholls, R. H., *Racing to Read*, Leeds, E. J. Arnold, 1962

Williamson A., and Leach, S. M., *Gay Colour Books*, Leeds, E. J. Arnold

4. DICTIONARIES

Devenport, P., *Pilot Dictionaries* (Pilot Reading Scheme), Leeds, E. J. Arnold, 1952

Noel, J., *Early Word Picture Dictionary*, London, Philip & Tacey, 1954; *Storymakers Picture Dictionary*, London, Philip & Tacey, 1955

5. NUMBER BOOKS

Austin, M. H., *Counting Time*, Edinburgh, McDougall

Bradbury, E. and L., *Read and Reckon Books*, 1–4, Oxford, Blackwell, 1959

Holland, D. A., *Oxford Graded Arithmetic*, London, Oxford University Press, 1958

Number Books, Leeds, E. J. Arnold, 1936

Schonell, F., *Practice in Basic Arithmetic*, Edinburgh, Oliver & Boyd, 1961

Taylor, A. (ed.), *New Nation Arithmetic*, London, Nelson, from 1953